Penny Haren's
PIECED APPLIQUÉ™
Weekend Projects

Landauer Books

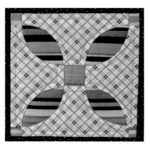

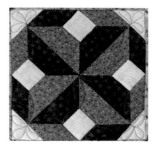

Penny Haren's
PIECED APPLIQUÉ
Weekend Projects

Copyright© 2009 by Landauer Corporation

Pieced Appliqué™ projects
Copyright© 2009 by Penny Haren

This book was designed, produced, and published by
Landauer Books
A division of Landauer Corporation
3100 101st Street, Urbandale, IA 50322
www.landauercorp.com   800/557-2144

President/Publisher: Jeramy Lanigan Landauer
Vice President of Sales and Operations: Kitty Jacobson
Managing Editor: Jeri Simon
Art Director: Laurel Albright
Photographer: Sue Voegtlin

ISBN 13: 978-0-9818040-4-0
ISBN 10:   0-9818040-4-7
Library of Congress Control Number: 2009927746

This book printed on acid-free paper.
Printed in U.S.A.

10-9-8-7-6-5-4-3-2-1

$\mathcal{L}$ike all quilters, I feel a great sense of accomplishment when I finish a project. That's why I love the small projects in this book. All can be finished in a day or a weekend—talk about instant gratification!

Have some fun and mix things up a bit. Substitute your favorite Pieced Appliqué™ blocks from my first two books into any of the project settings. Change the look by fussy cutting the center of your blocks or changing the color scheme. The possibilities are endless and I've included some examples to get your creative juices flowing.

After all, who would have thought the three blocks on the right all started with a simple nine-patch foundation - and every block can be finished in less than an hour! This is so much fun that you may spend more time picking out your fabrics – and fussy cutting – than you spend actually sewing.

This book would not have been possible without the help of some great friends. Barb Campolo spent many a night sewing with me into the wee hours of the morning – and then would take the project home to finish it. She "reverse sewed" a lot of seams when I changed my mind along the way and never whined—not once!

Cheryl Lorence is responsible for the beautiful machine quilting. Not only did she do heirloom quality quilting on every project, she also never complained when I gave her ridiculous deadlines and always made me look good!

And, the gals at Landauer are amazing. I have the best publisher in the industry and count my blessings every day! They make the whole process fun and have the ability to keep me focused—a full time job in itself. They believed in this technique—and me—from day one and have supported me every step of the way!

Get some friends together for a weekend and enjoy the fast, fun, and simple projects on the following pages. I guarantee you'll finish what you start!

Love,
Penny

Table of Contents

Benartex Fabrics by Nancy Halvorsen

Fabric by Mary Engelbreit®

Full Sun by Maywood Fabrics

1941
Nine-Patch
table topper 40

Benartex Fabrics by Nancy Halvorsen

Fabrics by LakeHouse Dry Goods

Cornerstone
table runner 44

Cornerstone
place mats 50

Fabrics by LakeHouse Dry Goods

Table of Contents

Fabrics by LakeHouse Dry Goods

Benartex Fabrics by Nancy Halvorsen

Henry Glass Fabrics by Buggy Barn

Shaded Trail
place mats 77

Henry Glass Fabrics by Buggy Barn

Fabric by Timeless Treasures and LakeHouse Dry Goods

Star of the East
table runner 84

Whirligigs
bulletin board 90

Fabrics by LakeHouse Dry Goods

General Instructions

Introducing Pieced Appliqué™

Pieced Appliqué™ is an innovative new technique to create traditional pieced blocks with more accuracy and ease than the current methods. Even a beginner can create complicated blocks—even miniature blocks—with excellent results.

With Pieced Appliqué™

- You see exactly what your finished block will look like before anything is stitched.
- You position and appliqué points and curves for perfect placement without machine piecing.
- You create blocks with very sharp points and curves that are impossible to achieve with traditional methods.
- You eliminate puckers created by piecing inset points and "Y" seams by appliquéing them.
- You can carry your blocks with you to work on wherever you go.

Creating Pieced Appliqué™ Blocks in 5 Easy Steps

1 **Create an easy foundation block**

2 **Make paper templates and iron on freezer paper**

3 **Glue the template to the wrong side of the fabric and turn with a glue stick**

4 **Stitch the appliqués to the foundation block to create the desired archival block**

5 **Remove the paper templates by soaking the block in warm water to dissolve the glue, then dry and press the completed block**

The Pieced Appliqué™ Process

Making the Foundation Blocks:
The first step in the Pieced Appliqué™ process is making your foundation block.

Making the Paper Templates:
To make the paper templates for your appliqués, either photocopy the template patterns shown with the block instructions or trace the template patterns onto white typing paper.

Note: *To download a complete set of templates for all the blocks in this book, in the multiples needed, visit www.landauercorp.com. Some printers will shrink these templates to fit preset margins. Run one copy and check it against the templates in the book to be sure they are printing at 100%.*

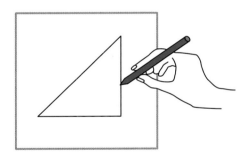

- **Adding the Freezer Paper:**
  Place the photocopied paper pattern face down on the ironing board so that any water in the iron does not smear the ink on the copy. Place the waxy side of the freezer paper on top of the **BLANK** side of the copied paper templates. Freezer paper is available at grocery stores in the paper products aisle or in 8-1/2" x 11" sheets at your local quilt shop.

TIP

Some copiers distort images more than others. Check your copies for accuracy by comparing your templates to the templates in the book. If your copier distorts the pattern too much, you will have to trace the pattern onto white typing paper or find another copier. My own copier tends to distort in one direction about 1/16". I can live with that.

Make sure that the ink from your copies will not bleed and discolor the fabric when wet. We have not had any problems with this yet, but there is always that chance. Better safe than sorry.

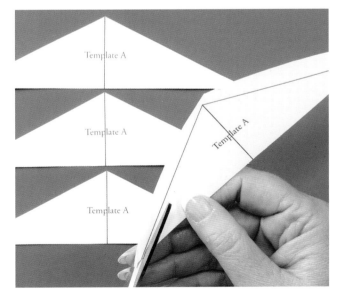

- **Cutting Out the Paper Templates:**
  When cutting out the paper templates, be sure to cut just **INSIDE** photocopied (or drawn) lines to allow for the thickness of the fabric when turning the fabric over the template to make the appliqué.

Preparing and Cutting the Fabric Appliqué

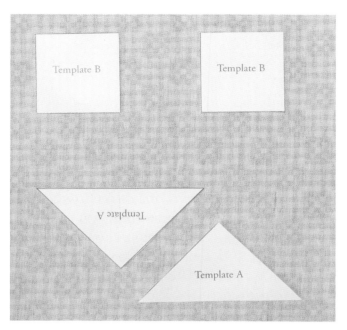

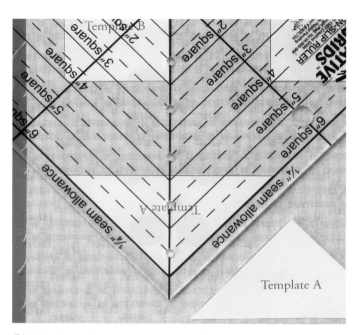

Glue the **BLANK** side of the freezer paper template onto the wrong side of the fabric. The printing on the freezer paper template should be face up.

Place the ruler on the template and measure to provide for a 1/4" seam allowance. Use a rotary cutter to trim the fabric exactly 1/4" away from the paper template on all sides. If you are using the Creative Grids™ *Square It Up & Fussy Cut* ruler, the 1/4" seam is marked for you.

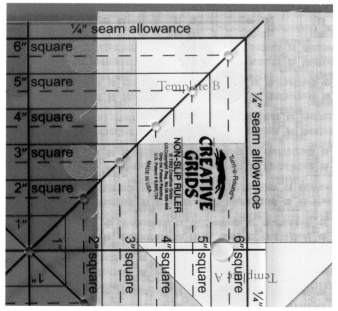

By placing the corner of the ruler on the template, you can trim two sides at once.

TIP

When you are told to trim the fabric exactly 1/4" away from the template, it is not a suggestion. By trimming 1/4" away, you are adding an accurate seam allowance to the appliqué which will help you position the appliqué on your foundation block. Since all curved sides are turned, you can estimate the 1/4" seam allowance on those edges.

Turning the Appliqués
Turning Straight Edges and Corners:

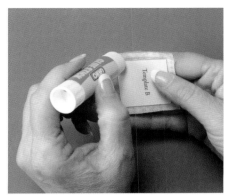

Run a glue stick along the edge of the paper template and the edge of the fabric to be turned. Be sure to run the glue past the template into the seam allowance.

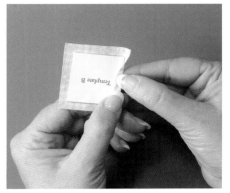

Turn the edge of the wrong side of the fabric over the template using your thumbnail and move forward 1/8" at a time. At the corner turn the fabric so it is angled slightly down.

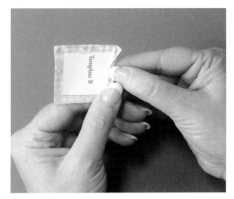

When the right angle is turned, the seam allowance for the second side will be totally hidden by the template.

Note: In block instructions the sides of the templates to be turned are marked with an ∗ Unturned sides are the seam allowances.

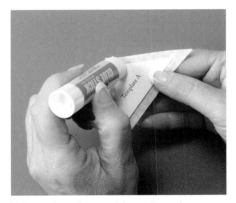

When turning a triangle, glue and turn the two sides just like a square.

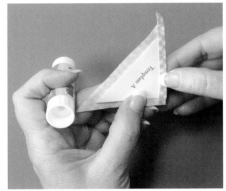

This will create "tails" on the bottom raw edge of the triangle.

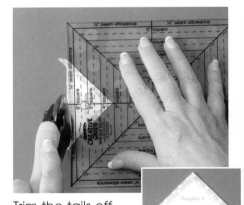

Trim the tails off even with the seam allowance.

TIP

I use white paste glue sticks to turn my appliqués. Don't purchase the purple, pink, and blue ones. You don't want to risk dyes coming back at a later date. Buy the large packages of glue sticks and keep them in the refrigerator. The moist environment stops them from drying out and they will last up to a year. When you are not using your glue stick, put the lid back on. They dry out very quickly if you leave the top off while turning each piece.

Turning the Appliqués

Turning Outside Curves:

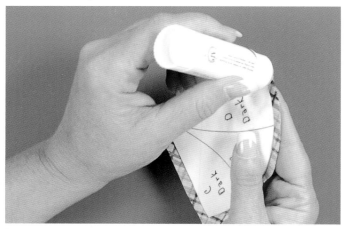

Some blocks have appliqués with curves. When turning an outside curve trim the fabric approximately 1/4" away from the curved side of the template. Turn and gather the fabric around the template. Do not clip outside curves. If you have rough edges on your appliqué, turn it over to the wrong side. You will notice there are pleats on the folded edge of your piece. While the glue is still wet, place a fingernail on each side of the "pleat" and pull it down to the correct shape. The straight edges should be trimmed exactly 1/4" away from the template.

Turning Inside Curves:

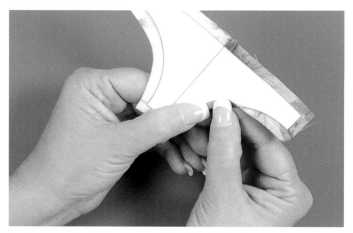

To turn an inside curve, trim the fabric approximately 1/4" away from the curved sides of the template. The inside curve of this appliqué does not have to be clipped. Since it is a gentle curve and the straight side of the template is placed on the grain line of the fabric, the curve is automatically placed on the bias and turns easily with no clipping required. The straight edges should be trimmed exactly 1/4" away from the template.

Turning Inner Circles:

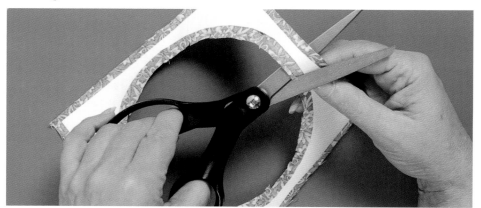

In the picture above, the center circle must be cut out approximately 1/4" away from the inner circle of the template. The seam allowance must be clipped in order to turn the fabric over the template. The straight edges should be trimmed exactly 1/4" away from the template.

Run a glue stick along the edge of the paper template and fabric. Turn the edge of the wrong side of the fabric over the template. Move your thumbnail forward 1/8" at a time.

Layering One Appliqué Over Another

Hand Appliqué

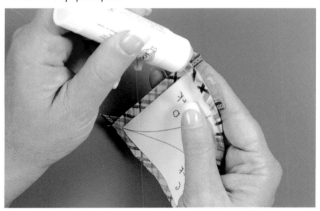

Some blocks require one appliqué to be placed on top of another. If you are going to hand appliqué, glue the wrong side of the top appliqué to the right side of the bottom appliqué.

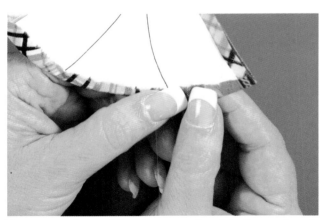

The raw edge of the top appliqué is then glued and turned over the edge of the bottom appliqué. When you hand appliqué, you will catch the fabric edges of both appliqués with your needle and thread while avoiding the paper template.

Machine Appliqué

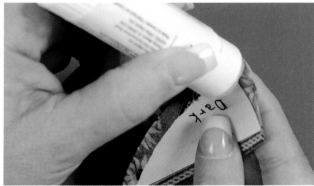

If you are going to machine appliqué, the appliqués must be glued to the foundation block and sewn, one layer at a time, so the templates can be removed before the next layer of appliqués is stitched in place. You do not want to sew the templates into your finished block. Continue to machine appliqué and remove the templates, one layer at a time, until the block is complete.

Turn all pieces before appliquéing any in place to ensure that subsequent layers of appliqués will cover and match the layer below it.

TIP

Clip inside points and curves to within a few threads of the template to aid in turning. Do not clip outside curves. Every cut is a potential weakness in your project.

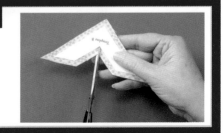

Cutting Appliqués from a Pieced Block

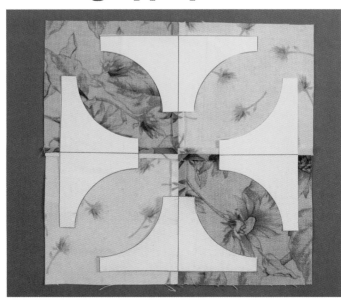

Some of the Pieced Appliqué™ blocks require two foundation blocks. One of the blocks will be used to cut the appliqués, as demonstrated in the photo above. Place the lines of the paper template on the seam lines of the wrong side of the pieced block and trim 1/4" away from the templates on all sides.

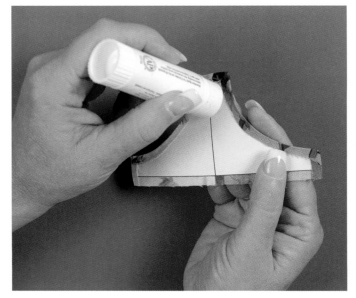

Glue and turn the sides of the appliqué as instructed in the block directions. In the picture above, the inside curve of the appliqué does not have to be clipped. Since it is a gentle curve and the straight side of the template is placed on the grain line of the fabric, the curve is automatically placed on the bias and turns easily.

Run glue on the wrong side of the template. Match the seam lines of the appliqué to the seam lines of the foundation block and glue in place. Do not place glue on the seam allowance. You don't want to stitch through it later.

Rotate the block as you place the appliqués. Since the appliqués were trimmed exactly 1/4" away from the templates, place the raw edges even with the raw edges of the foundation block.

Stitching the Appliqué Templates
Thread
Use only high quality cotton thread or cotton wrapped polyester. Not all threads are created equal.

 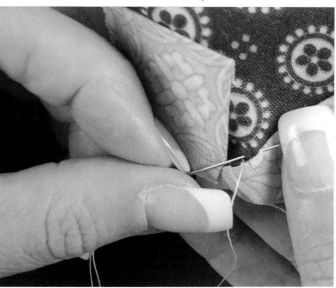

Hand stitch the turned edges of the appliqué, using an invisible appliqué stitch. Leave the raw edges open. If your appliquéd pieces are layered, only stitch to the fabric directly below. Do not go clear down to the foundation block. You don't want to sew the paper templates into your work. Take a few extra stitches to reinforce any areas that were clipped because of inside curves. Knots should be hidden beneath the appliqué piece. Do not place your knot on the wrong side of the foundation square. The thread tail could shadow through the finished block.

If you prefer to machine stitch, use a narrow zigzag stitch with invisible thread in the top of your machine and 50 or 60 weight thread in the bobbin. If your appliqué pieces are layered, stitch the bottom appliqué first. Remove the paper templates and press your block. Glue the second layer of appliqués to your block and stitch them in place. Remove the paper templates and glue, following directions on pages 16-17.

Removing the Paper Templates and Glue

When the stitching is done, place the appliquéd block into warm water for at least twenty minutes. This will dissolve the glue.

Remove the appliquéd block from the water and squeeze out the excess water.

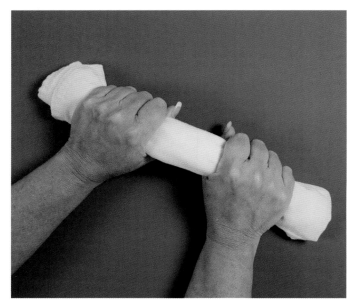

Roll the block in an absorbent towel to remove any remaining water.

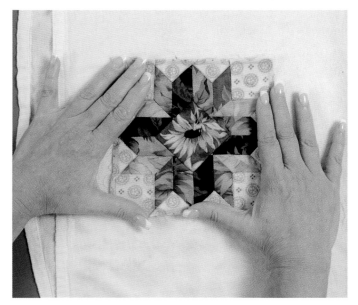

Smooth the block out on the towel and let dry before removing the paper templates.

TIP

Place several completed blocks in a sink of warm water before going to bed and remove them in the morning. If you are afraid the fabrics may bleed, add a color grabber sheet.

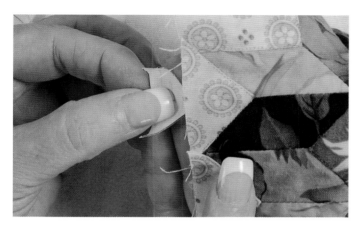

Pull out the paper templates along the raw edges of the block. If necessary, run the seams under water to flush out any remaining glue.

To remove inside templates, slit or cut the background fabric. Avoid cutting through the appliquéd stitches

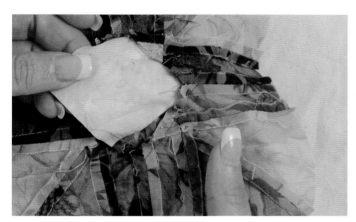

Remove the inside paper templates. Cut away any excess fabric if you are going to hand appliqué or the foundation block will shadow through the completed block.

Smooth the block out again and press.

TIP

Press the seams open when sewing your foundation block to evenly distribute the bulk of the fabric in the seam allowance.

TIP

Press your appliquéd blocks on a folded bath towel. The towel absorbs the seams so that there is no "shadow" created by the seams on the front of the piece. Spray each piece with spray starch and press the wrong side to guarantee that all of the seams are pressed correctly. Then press the right side. The spray starch gives it a crisp look, reduces distortion and fraying, and protects the finished block.

Fussy Cutting

Many of the appliqués can be fussy cut to showcase a particular design in the fabric. This technique adds drama and eye appeal to the Pieced Appliqué™ blocks. The Creative Grids™ *Square It Up & Fussy Cut* ruler makes the process quick and easy. This ruler consists of squares drawn symmetrically around a center hole. These symmetrical squares are drawn with solid black lines at 1" increments. Squares are drawn with black dashed lines at the 1/2" increments starting with 1-1/2". Holes are drilled at the center and at the corners of the dashed squares drawn at the 1/2" increments beginning with the 1-1/2" square.

These holes are drilled so that a water soluble pen or chalk pencil can be inserted to mark the fabric underneath. By marking the fabric through these holes, a 1/4" seam allowance is automatically added to the piece.

PLACE THE RULER AND MARK YOUR FABRIC

Place the ruler over the design you want to fussy cut. In this case, the ruler is placed over a sunflower. The sunflower is centered within the 2" solid black square. A chalk pencil is used to mark the corner of the dashed square at 2-1/2". This automatically adds the seam allowance to that piece. When cut, the sunflower will be in the exact center of the square.

FUSSY CUT THE DESIGN

Remove the ruler and use it to draw lines that connect the marked dots on the fabric. Cut out the fabric square on the drawn line.

ADD THE PAPER TEMPLATE

The fussy cut square is now ready to have the paper template glued to the wrong side of the fabric.

TIP

Triangles can be fussy cut by marking the corner and points of the triangle. Trim the two straight sides; cut the diagonal.

Introducing Foundation Blocks

Every finished Pieced Appliqué™ block is built on an easy-to-make foundation block. The name of the foundation block you need to make for each finished block is given at the beginning of the instructions.

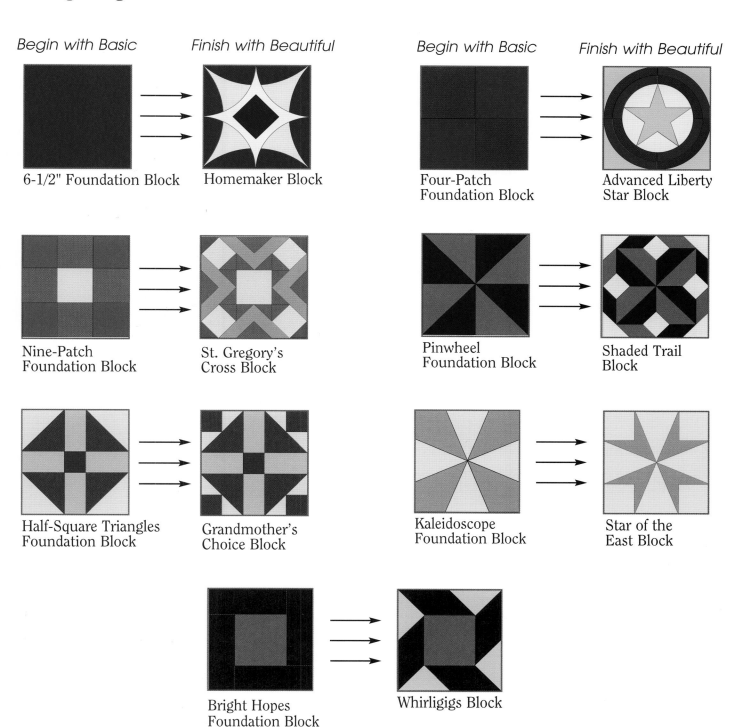

Begin with Basic → *Finish with Beautiful*

6-1/2" Foundation Block → Homemaker Block

Begin with Basic → *Finish with Beautiful*

Four-Patch Foundation Block → Advanced Liberty Star Block

Nine-Patch Foundation Block → St. Gregory's Cross Block

Pinwheel Foundation Block → Shaded Trail Block

Half-Square Triangles Foundation Block → Grandmother's Choice Block

Kaleidoscope Foundation Block → Star of the East Block

Bright Hopes Foundation Block → Whirligigs Block

Homemaker
table runner
14-1/2" x 34"

Perfect points are a breeze with Penny Haren's
Pieced Appliqué™ technique and no inset seams.

Designed & pieced by Penny Haren. Machine quilted by Cheryl Lorence.

Fabrics

Light Cream Print Fabric:
Fat quarter for
Pieced Appliqué™ blocks

Medium Gold Print Fabric:
Fat quarter for
Pieced Appliqué™ blocks

Medium Red Print Fabric:
1 yard for Pieced Appliqué™
blocks, yo-yos, and backing

Dark Red Print Fabric:
Scraps for Pieced Appliqué™
blocks

Dark Green Print Fabric:
1/3 yard for
border and binding

**Cardboard or Template Plastic
for yo-yos**

*Refer to General Instructions on pages 8-19
before beginning this project.*

Note: *All yardage requirements are
based on 44"-wide fabric, NOT pre-washed.
Measurements include 1/4" seam allowance.*

*Homemaker
Pieced Appliqué™ Blocks*

Cutting

Light Cream Print Fabric:
Cut 3—6-1/2" Squares

Medium Gold Print Fabric:
Cut 12 of Appliqué B

Medium Red Print Fabric:
Cut 12 of Appliqué C and
12 of Appliqué D

Dark Red Print Fabric:
Cut 3 of Appliqué A

Paper Templates:
Cut 3 of Template A and
12 of Templates B, C, and D

**Make 3—Homemaker
Pieced Appliqué™ Blocks**

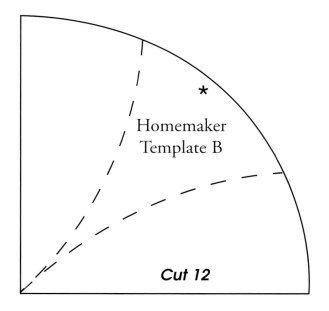

Homemaker
Template B

Cut 12

Homemaker
Template A

Cut 3

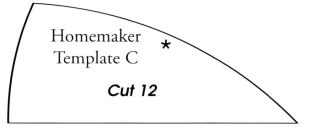

Homemaker
Template C

Cut 12

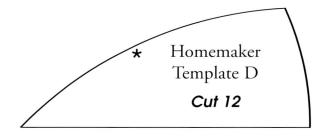

Homemaker
Template D

Cut 12

Backing & Binding

Cutting

Medium Red Print Fabric:
Cut 2—8" squares for backing
of 2 blocks
Cut 1—12" square for backing
of the center block

Dark Green Print Fabric:
Cut 3—1-1/2" strips for binding

Note: I gave all three blocks and a 1/2 yard of backing fabric to my machine quilter. She quilted all three blocks to the same backing fabric so it was easier to attach to her quilting machine. Ask your machine quilter how she would like you to prepare the pieces.

1. Layer backing, batting, and blocks. Quilt the blocks as desired.

2. Use a single fold binding to eliminate bulk in this small project.

Yo-Yos

Cutting

Cardboard or Template Plastic:
Cut a 3-3/4" circular template
(measurement includes a scant
1/4" seam allowance)

Medium Red Print Fabric:
Cut 66 circles using
yo-yo template

Note: You may choose to use the large Clover Yo-Yo Maker to make the yo-yos. Follow the instructions included with the Yo-Yo- Maker.

1. Thread a hand-sewing needle with matching quilting thread and knot the thread. With the wrong side of one fabric circle facing you, turn up the seam allowance and bring the needle down through both layers of the fabric. Sew running stitches around the circle, folding up the seam allowance as you go. When you are back to the starting point, tug on

the thread to gather the fabric into a yo-yo; secure the thread with a few backstitches. Press the yo-yo flat.

Attaching the Yo-yo's

1. Beginning with the bordered Homemaker block, pin a yo-yo to each corner. Evenly distribute six yo-yos along one edge between two corner yo-yos, making sure they fit nicely next to each other.

Note: If the yo-yos seem crowded or overlap you may wish to make slightly smaller corner yo-yos.

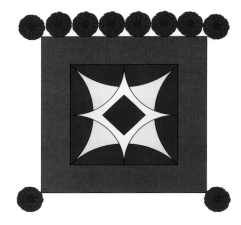

2. Tack the yo-yos to the binding and to each other. Repeat on the remaining sides of the bordered Homemaker block.

3 Repeat this process for the two smaller blocks, omitting one corner yo-yo from each block.

4 To assemble the table runner, position a small block at opposite corners of the large block, sharing the corner yo-yos. Tack in place.

Note: *For extra stability, tack together the yo-yos on either side of the shared corner yo-yos.*

Yo-Yo Template

Homemaker
table runner

True Lover's Knot
table square
24-1/2" x 24-1/2"

*Play with prints to see how different fabrics
create a colorful contrast against a 6-1/2" striped fabric square.*

Designed & pieced by Sue Voegtlin. Machine quilted by Lynn Witzenburg.

Fabrics

Multi-Stripe Print Fabric:
1/2 yard for
Pieced Appliqué™ blocks

Assorted Print Fabrics:
4-5 Fat quarters for Pieced
Appliqué™ blocks
(use more for a scrappier look)

Black Dot Print Fabric:
1-1/4 yards for sashing, border,
and backing

Medium Red Print Fabric:
1/4 yard for binding

*Refer to General Instructions on pages 8-19
before beginning this project.*

Note: *All yardage requirements
are based on 44"-wide fabric,
NOT pre-washed. Measurements include
1/4" seam allowance.*

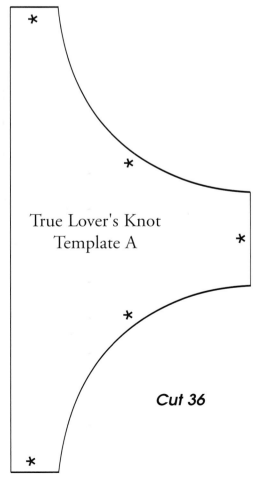

True Lover's Knot
Template A

Cut 36

True Lover's Knot
Pieced Appliqué™ Blocks

Cutting

Multi-Stripe Print Fabric:
Cut 9—6-1/2" Squares

Assorted Print Fabrics:
Cut 36 of Appliqué A—4 each from
matching fabrics

Paper Templates:
Cut 36 of Template A

**Make 9—True Lover's Knot
Pieced Appliqué™ Blocks**

Piecing
This block consists of 5 pieces.

1 Glue four A paper templates to the
wrong side of an assorted print fabric.

2 Trim the fabric EXACTLY 1/4" away from
the straight sides of each template. Trim
the fabric approximately 1/4" away from
the curved edges. Do not turn the long
straight side of each template. Turn all
other edges.

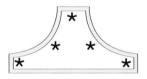

Template A

Note: * *on paper templates indicates
sides of fabric to be turned.*

3 Glue the wrong side of the appliqués in
place on the multi-stripe 6-1/2" squares.
The raw edges of the appliqués should
be placed even with the raw edges of
the 6-1/2" square.

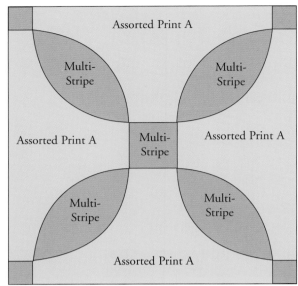

Assorted Print A

Multi-Stripe
Multi-Stripe

Assorted Print A
Multi-Stripe
Assorted Print A

Multi-Stripe
Multi-Stripe

Assorted Print A

4 Appliqué in place, leaving the raw edges open. Follow directions on pages 16-17 to remove paper templates and glue. Press.

5 Repeat Steps 1-4 to make a total of nine True Lover's Knot blocks.

Sashing & Border

Cutting

Black Dot Print Fabric:

Cut 1—2" strip for sashing
   Sub-cut into 6—6-1/2" strips

Cut 2—2" x 21-1/2" strips for sashing

Cut 2—2" x 21-1/2" strips for the top and bottom borders

Cut 2—2" x 24-1/2" strips for the side borders

1 Lay out three True Lover's Knot Pieced Appliqué™ blocks and two 6-1/2" sashing strips. Sew together to make one row. Repeat to make a total of three rows.

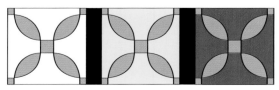

Make 3

2 Lay out the three block rows and the two 2" x 21-1/2" sashing strips, as shown. Sew together to form the table square center.

3 Sew a 2" x 21-1/2" border strip to the top and bottom edges of the table square center. Trim the border strips even with the table square center.

4 Sew a 2" x 24-1/2" border strips to each side of the table square center. Trim the side border strips even with the table topper center.

Backing & Binding

Cutting

Black Dot Print Fabric:
Cut 1—30" square for backing

Medium Red Print Fabric:
Cut 3—2-1/4" strips for binding

1 Layer backing, batting, and table topper center. Quilt and bind as desired.

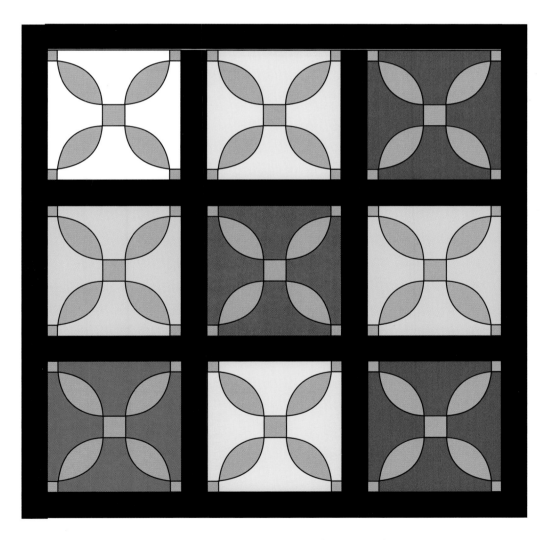

True Lover's Knot
table square

Four-Patch Foundation Block _____

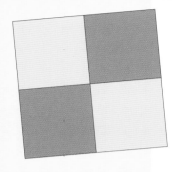

A four-patch is a block that consists of four squares of equal size.

Two squares of contrasting fabrics will make two four-patches. The squares must be cut at least 1" larger than the finished size of the block.

If you need a 6" finished four-patch, for instance, cut the squares at least 7". After sewing, the four-patches should measure 6-1/2". This includes the seam allowances.

I prefer to cut the squares 2" larger so that I can trim the four-patches to the correct size after the sewing is complete. In some cases, they are cut even larger so appliqués can be cut from the pieced block.

Fabrics

Cut 1—8" Square of
a Light Fabric

Cut 1—8" Square of
a Dark Fabric

Piecing

1 Place the light fabric square, right sides together, on top of the dark fabric square.

Note: *Use spray starch to iron the squares together.*

2 Sew a 1/4" seam along two opposite sides of the squares using a matching cotton thread. Clip all threads.

3 Cut this unit in half, parallel to the sewn seams. Each strip should measure 4". Press the seams open.

4 Place these two units, right sides together, with the dark fabric strip on top of the light fabric strip. Match the seams.

5 To ensure the center seams of the four-patches match perfectly, place a dab of glue to hold them in place. Fold back the top unit about an inch and line up the seams. Do not place any glue 1/4" in from the edge or you will glue the seam allowance closed and will not be able to press it open later. Any dab of glue that shows on the front of the block will disappear when the templates are removed.

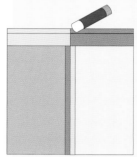

6 Sew a 1/4" seam along the two opposite sides that are perpendicular to the sewn seams.

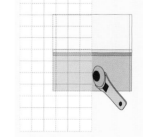

7 Cut this unit in half, parallel to the sewn seams. Each strip should measure 4". Press the seams open.

8 Place the 6-1/2" Creative Grids™ *Square It Up & Fussy Cut* ruler on top of the four-patch, placing the horizontal and vertical lines on the seam lines of the four-patch. Trim the outside edge of the block.

Note: *In most cases, one four-patch will be used as the foundation block and will be trimmed to 6-1/2". Trim the one with the perfect center. Appliqués will be cut from the other four-patch, so the center will be cut away. Do NOT trim the second four-patch. It is over-sized so that the appliqués can be cut from it.*

You now have two completed four-patch units.

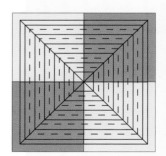

Advanced *Liberty Star*
table runner
16-1/2" x 28-1/2"

Even a beginner can successfully create this block using Pieced Appliqué™ techniques for flawless points and curves. Use this simple setting to try optional blocks and colorways.

Designed & pieced by Penny Haren. Machine quilted by Cheryl Lorence.

Fabrics

Light Gold Print
Fat quarter for
Pieced Appliqué™ blocks

Medium Gold Print
Scrap or fat quarter for
Pieced Appliqué™ blocks

Light Cream Print
Scrap or fat quarter for
Pieced Appliqué™ blocks

Medium Red Print
Scrap or fat quarter for
Pieced Appliqué™ blocks

Medium Blue Print
1/2 yard for Pieced Appliqué™
blocks and backing

Dark Blue Print
1/3 yard for outer border

Dark Red Print
1/2 yard for inner border
and binding

*Refer to General Instructions on pages 8-19
before beginning this project.*

*Note: All yardage requirements
are based on 44"-wide fabric,
NOT pre-washed. Measurements
include 1/4" seam allowance.*

The paper templates are glued to the wrong side of the fabric. Therefore, the turned appliqué is a mirror image of the original template. In this case, the A & B templates and the C & D templates are mirror images of each other. The templates provided have been reversed for you.

Note: If you are going to machine appliqué the block, see instructions on page 15. These instructions are written for hand appliqué.

Advanced Liberty Star Pieced Appliqué™ Blocks

Cutting

Light Gold Print Fabric:
Cut 2—6-1/2" squares

Medium Gold Print Fabric:
Cut 1—6-1/2" square

Light Cream Print Fabric:
Cut three of Appliqués A, B, C, D, and E

Medium Red Print Fabric:
Cut 3—8" squares

Medium Blue Print Fabric:
Cut 3—8" squares

Paper Templates:
Cut 3 of Templates A, B, C, D, and E
Cut 3 of Templates F, G, and H

**Make 3—Advanced Liberty Star
Pieced Appliqué™ Blocks**

Piecing

This block consists of 14 pieces.

1. Following the four-patch foundation block directions on page 30, make six four-patches with the 8" medium red print fabric squares and the 8" medium blue print fabric squares. The finished four-patches are oversized—they should measure approximately 7-1/2". The centers won't show in the finished block.

2. Glue the A, B, C, D, and E paper templates to the wrong side of the light cream print fabric. Trim the fabric EXACTLY 1/4" away from the sides of

each template. Turn the two straight sides of each appliqué. Do not turn the curved edges.

Note: * on paper templates indicate sides of fabric to be turned.

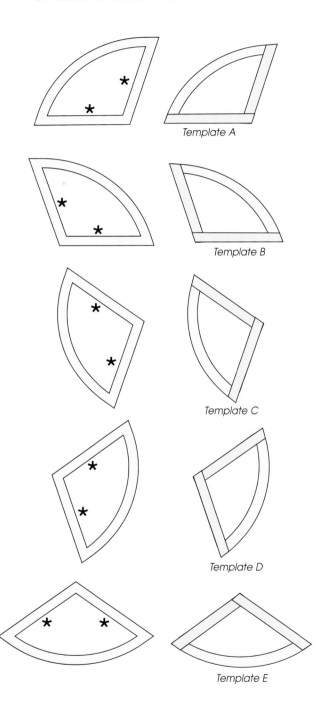

Template A

Template B

Template C

Template D

Template E

3 With a water soluble marker, draw a vertical and horizontal line through the 6-1/2" light and medium gold print

fabric squares. Use these lines to aid in placing the appliqué pieces.

4 Center and glue an F template to the right side of the light and medium gold print fabric squares. The top point of the star should be placed 1-1/4" from the top edge of the square on the drawn vertical line. This template is used to aid in placement only. It will be removed when the A, B, C, D, and E appliqués are glued in place.

5 Glue the wrong side of the A, B, C, D, and E appliqués in place on the right sides of the 6-1/2" light and medium gold print fabric squares. The turned sides of the appliqués should be placed even with the F paper template. Remove the F template.

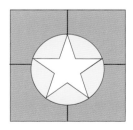
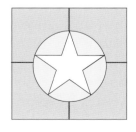

6 Glue the G paper templates to the wrong side of three of the four-patch units, matching the drawn lines on the templates to the seam lines on the four-patches. Trim the fabric 1/4" away

from the inner and outer circles of the templates. Clip and turn the inner circles.

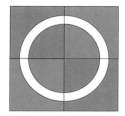 

7 Center and glue the G appliqués in place on the light and medium gold print fabric squares. Place the seam lines of the appliqués on the drawn horizontal and vertical lines of the fabric squares. The turned inner circle of this appliqué will cover the raw, curved edges of the appliqués that form the star.

8 Glue the H paper templates to the wrong side of the remaining four-patch squares, matching the drawn lines on the templates to the seam lines on the four-patches. Trim the fabric 1/4" away from the inner and outer circles of the templates. Clip and turn both the inner and outer circles.

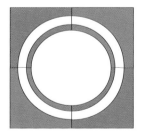 

9 Center and glue the H appliqués in place over the G appliqués. Place the seam lines of the appliqués on the drawn horizontal and vertical lines. The turned inner circle of this appliqué will cover the raw edges of the G appliqués.

10 Appliqué in place, leaving the raw edges open. Follow directions on pages 16-17 to remove paper templates and glue. Press.

11 Lay out the three Advanced Liberty Star blocks, as shown. Sew together to form the table runner center.

Borders

Cutting

Dark Red Print Fabric:
Cut 2—1-1/2" x 8-1/2" strips for the inner border
Cut 2—1-1/2" x 18-1/2" strips for the inner border

Dark Blue Print Fabric:
Cut 2—4-1/2" x 20-1/2" strips for the outer border
Cut 2—4-1/2" x 16-1/2" strips for the outer border

1 Sew a 1-1/2" x 18-1/2" dark red print strip to the top and bottom edges of the table runner center.

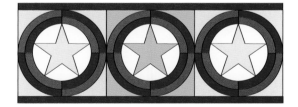

2 Sew a 1-1/2" x 8-1/2" dark red print strip to the side edges of the table runner center.

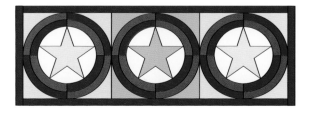

3 Sew a 4-1/2" x 20-1/2" dark blue print strip to the top and bottom edges of the table runner center.

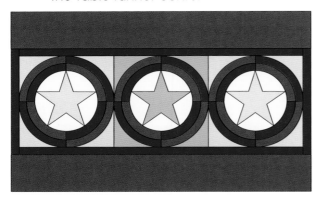

4 Sew a 4-1/2" x 16-1/2" dark blue print strip to the side edges of the table runner center.

Backing & Binding

Cutting

Medium Blue Print Fabric:
Cut 1—24" x 34" rectangle for backing

Dark Red Print Fabric:
Cut 3—2-1/2" strips to bind a straight border

Note: If you are cutting a scalloped edge, cut a single fold bias strip approximately 98" long..

1 Layer the runner top, batting and backing. Quilt as desired.

2 Trim the outer edges even or scallop, as shown in the diagram. Bind the runner.

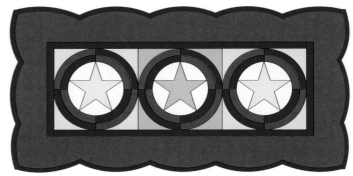

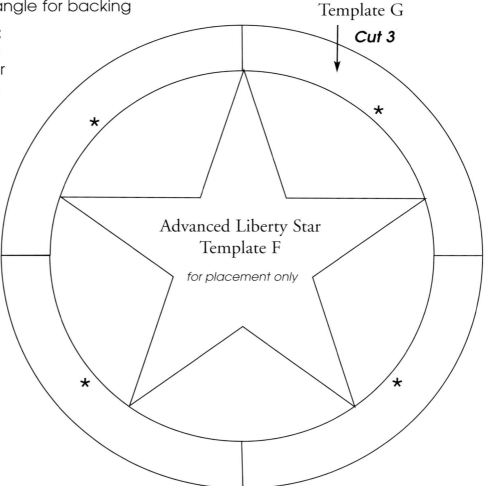

Advanced Liberty Star
Template G

Cut 3

Advanced Liberty Star
Template F

for placement only

table runner block and color option

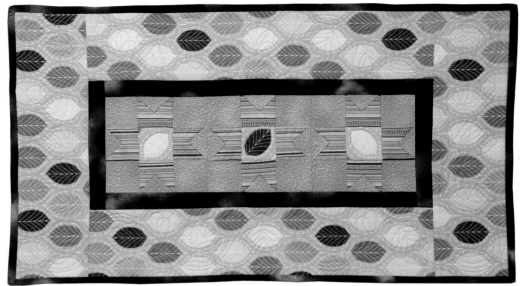

Pieced by Jeri Simon; machine quilted by Lynn Witzenburg.

Substitute your favorite Pieced Appliqué™ block in the Advanced Liberty Star Table Runner. We used the 1941 Nine-Patch on page 40.

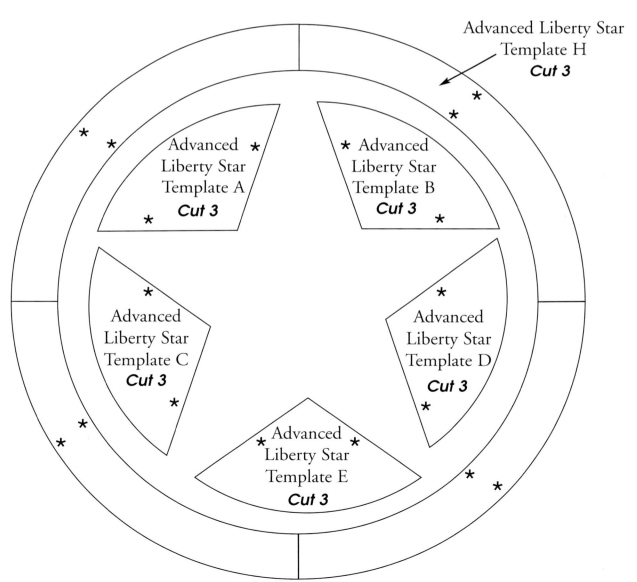

Advanced Liberty Star Template H
Cut 3

Advanced Liberty Star Template A
Cut 3

Advanced Liberty Star Template B
Cut 3

Advanced Liberty Star Template C
Cut 3

Advanced Liberty Star Template D
Cut 3

Advanced Liberty Star Template E
Cut 3

Nine-Patch Foundation Block

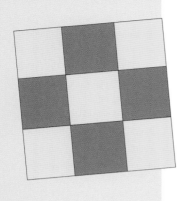

A nine-patch block traditionally consists of nine squares sewn in three rows of three squares.

In this book, a nine-patch consists of three rows of three units. Those nine units may consist of rectangles, half-square triangles, and even nine-patches. The method is the same.

Make a sample block to learn the technique before cutting the fabric for your quilt. Measure the completed block to check your seam allowance.

The completed block should measure 6-1/2".

FABRICS

5—2-1/2" Squares of Light Fabric

4—2-1/2" Squares of Dark Fabric

PIECING

1 Lay out the nine squares in three rows of three blocks each. In this example, the light fabric squares are placed at the corners and in the center. Follow each Pieced Appliqué™ block's directions for fabric placement.

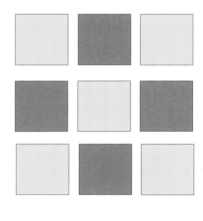

2 Place the squares in the center column – right sides together on the squares in the left-hand column. Pick up the first pair in the top left corner. Then, pick up the middle pair, then the bottom pair. The bottom pair of squares will be on the bottom of the stack. Pick up the right-hand column of squares from the top to the bottom in the same manner.

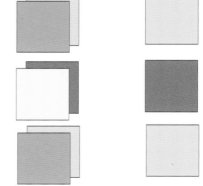

3 Pick up the top two squares, which are already right sides together, and sew the right side of the squares. Do not break the thread. Pick up the next two squares and sew the right side of these squares. Do not break the thread. Pick up the last two squares that are right sides together and sew the right side of these squares. Three squares will be left. The top square will be right side up. You have sewn three sets of two squares that are held together by threads.

4 Open the first set of squares and place the top, light square, right sides together, on the dark fabric square. Sew on the right side of the square. Do not break the thread.

5 Open the second set of squares and place the next, dark square, right sides together, on the light fabric square. Sew on the right side of the square. Do not break the thread.

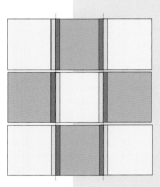

6 Open the third set of squares and place the remaining light square, right sides together, on the dark fabric square. Sew on the right side of the square. Do not clip the thread. The threads will hold the rows together so you don't lose any pieces and act as pins when sewing the rows togther. Press the seams open.

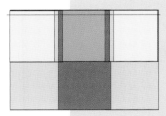

7 Place the second row, right sides together, on the first row, matching the seams. Place a dab of glue on these seams so everything matches perfectly. Place the third row, right sides together, on the second row. Match the seams and sew this seam.

8 Clip the threads that held the rows together and press the seams open.

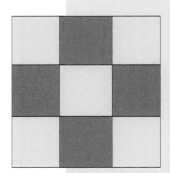

1941 Nine-Patch
table topper
39-1/2" x 39-1/2"

Repeat a favorite Pieced Appliqué™ block and see how easy it is to create a beautiful holiday table topper.

Designed by Penny Haren; pieced by Barb Campolo. Machine quilted by Cheryl Lorence.

Fabrics

Light Brown Print Fabric:
1 yard for Pieced Appliqué™ blocks and Snowball blocks

Medium Red Print Fabric:
2/3 yard for sashing

Dark Red Print Fabric:
1/8 yard or a 2-1/2" strip for Pieced Appliqué™ blocks

Dark Green Print Fabric:
1 yard for Pieced Appliqué™ blocks, Snowball blocks, and binding

Medium Print Fabric:
1-1/4 yards for backing

Refer to General Instructions on pages 8-19 before beginning this project.

Note: *All yardage requirements are based on 44"-wide fabric, NOT pre-washed. Measurements include 1/4" seam allowance.*

1941 Nine-Patch
Pieced Appliqué™ Blocks

Cutting

Light Brown Print Fabric:
#1—Cut 52—2-1/2" Squares
Scraps to Cut 62 of Appliqué A

Dark Red Print Fabric:
#2—Cut 13—2-1/2" Squares

Dark Green Print Fabric:
#3—Cut 52—2-1/2" Squares

Paper Templates:
Cut 52 of Template A

Make 13—1941 Nine-Patch Pieced Appliqué™ Blocks

Note: *You may choose to strip piece the nine-patches in this book. I chose to cut the squares individually since three fabrics are incorporated into the completed nine-patch. By cutting the squares individually, I could fussy cut them.*

Piecing
This block consists of 13 pieces.

1 Following the nine-patch foundation block directions on page 38, make a nine-patch with the #2 dark red print square (center); the #1 light brown print squares (corners); and the #3 dark green print squares. Press the seams open.

2 Glue the A paper templates to the wrong side of a scrap of light brown print fabric. Trim the fabric EXACTLY 1/4" away from all sides of each template.
Do not turn the longest side of each template. Turn the other two sides.
Note: ★ *on paper templates indicates sides of fabric to be turned.*

Template A

1941
Nine-Patch
★ Template A ★
Cut 52

3 Glue the wrong side of the appliqués in place on the pieced nine-patch block. The raw edge of the appliqués should be placed even with the raw edge of the block.

4 Appliqué in place, leaving raw edges open. Follow directions on pages 16-17 to remove paper templates and glue. Press.

5 Repeat Steps 1 - 4 to make a total of 13 1941 Nine-Patch Pieced Appliqué™ blocks.

#1 Light	Light A	#1 Light
	#3 Dark	
#3 Dark	#2 Dark	#3 Dark
Light A		Light A
	#3 Dark	
#1 Light	Light A	#1 Light

Snowball Setting Blocks

Cutting

Light Brown Print Fabric:
Cut 2—6-1/2" strips
Sub-cut into
12—6-1/2" squares

Dark Green Print Fabric:
Cut 3—2-1/2" strips
Sub-cut into
48—2-1/2" squares

Make 12 Snowball Setting Blocks

1 Using a chalk pencil, lightly draw a diagonal line on the wrong side of each dark green print square.

2 With right sides together and edges matching, place a dark green print square on one corner of a light brown print square. Sew diagonally across the small square. Repeat for the remaining three corners.

3 Trim each corner through both layers, leaving a 1/4-inch seam allowance Flip the corner triangles up and press.

4 Repeat Steps 1 - 3 to make a total of 12 Snowball Setting blocks.

Make 12

Sashing & Corner Squares

Cutting

Medium Red Print Fabric:
Cut 10—2" strips
Sub-cut into
60—6-1/2" sashing strips

Dark Green Print Fabric:
Cut 2—2" strips
Sub-cut into
36—2" corner squares

1 Lay out three 1941 Nine-Patch Pieced Appliqué™ blocks, two Snowball blocks, and six 6-1/2" sashing strips as shown. Sew together to make one row. Repeat to make a total of three rows.

Make 3

2 Lay out three Snowball blocks, two 1941 Nine-Patch Pieced Appliqué™ blocks, and six 6-1/2" sashing strips as shown. Sew together to make one row. Repeat to make a total of two rows.

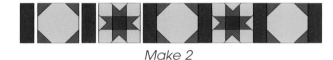

Make 2

3 Lay out five 6-1/2" sashing strips and six 2" corner squares, as shown, to create one long sashing strip. Sew together. Repeat to make a total of six long sashing strips.

Make 6

4 To assemble the quilt top, join the long sashing strips and block rows, as shown.

Backing & Binding

Cutting

Medium Print Fabric:
Cut 1—45" square for backing

Dark Green Print Fabric:
Cut 5—2-1/4" strips for binding

1 Layer the table topper top, batting, and backing. Quilt and bind as desired.

1941 Nine-Patch
table topper

Cornerstone
table runner
18-1/2" x 42-1/2"

*You'll love how easy it is to appliqué
a mitered corner—even with matching stripes.*

Designed by Penny Haren; pieced by Barb Campolo. Machine quilted by Cheryl Lorence.

Fabrics

Light Floral Print Fabric:
Scrap or Fat quarter for
Pieced Appliqué™ blocks

Light Print Fabric:
1/4 yard for sashing strips

Medium Blue Print Fabric:
Scrap or Fat quarter for
Pieced Appliqué™ blocks

Medium Floral Print Fabric:
1-1/3 yards for Pieced Appliqué™
blocks and backing

Medium Green Print Fabric:
1/2 yard for sashing strips and
four-patch squares

Dark Blue Print Fabric:
1/2 yard for four-patch squares
and binding

Dark Green Print Fabric:
Fat quarter for
Pieced Appliqué™ blocks

*Refer to General Instructions on pages 8-19
before beginning this project.*

*Note: All yardage requirements
are based on 44"-wide fabric,
NOT pre-washed. Measurements include
1/4" seam allowance.*

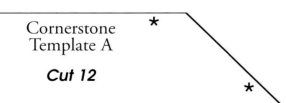

Cornerstone
Template A

Cut 12

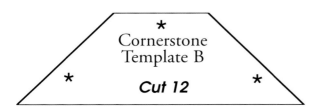

Cornerstone
Template B

Cut 12

Cornerstone Pieced Appliqué™ Blocks

Cutting

Light Floral Print Fabric:
#1—Cut 12—2-1/2" Squares

Medium Blue Print Fabric:
#2—Cut 12—2-1/2" Square

Medium Floral Print Fabric:
#3—Cut 3—2-1/2" Squares

Dark Green Print Fabric:
Cut 12 of Appliqué A and
12 of Appliqué B

Paper Templates:
Cut 12 of Template A and
12 of Template B

**Make 3—Cornerstone
Pieced Appliqué™ Blocks**

Piecing

This block consists of 17 pieces.

> **Note:** *The paper templates are glued
> to the wrong side of the fabric. The
> templates have been reversed for you.*
> **Note:** *I chose to fussy cut the center and
> corner squares. Fussy cutting adds drama
> to this block.*

1. Following the nine-patch foundation
block directions on page 38, make a
nine-patch with the #1 light floral print
squares (corners); the #3 medium floral
print square (center); and the #2
medium blue print squares. Press the
seams open.

2 Glue the A paper templates to the wrong side of a scrap of dark print fabric. Trim the fabric EXACTLY 1/4" away from the templates on all sides. Turn the two sides of each appliqué marked with an * on the template. Do not turn the other sides.

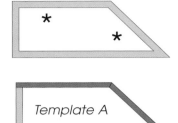

Template A

3 Glue the wrong side of the appliqués in place on the pieced nine-patch block. Place the raw edge of the appliqués even with the raw edge of the block.

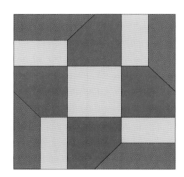

4 Glue the B paper templates to the wrong side of a scrap of dark print fabric. Trim the fabric EXACTLY 1/4" away from the templates on all sides. Turn the three shortest sides of each appliqué marked with an * on the template. Do not turn the longest side.

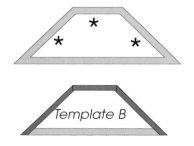

Template B

5 Glue the wrong side of the appliqués in place on the nine-patch foundation block.

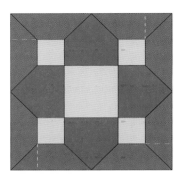

6 Appliqué in place, leaving the raw edges open. Follow directions on pages 16-17 to remove paper templates and glue. Press.

7 Repeat Steps 1-6 to make a total of 3 Cornerstone blocks.

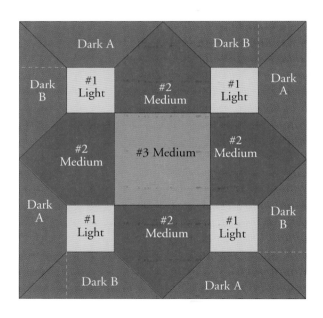

Four-Patch Squares

Cutting

Medium Green Print Fabric:
Cut 3—2" strips

Dark Blue Print Fabric:
Cut 3—2" strips

Make 28 Four-Patch Squares

Each Cornerstone block is framed with four sashing strips and a four-patch square in each corner. The three framed block units make up the center of the runner.

1 Sew a 2"-wide dark blue print strip to a 2"-wide medium green print strip to make one strip set. Repeat to make a total of three strip sets.

Make 3

2 Cut each strip set into 2"-wide units for a total of 56 units.

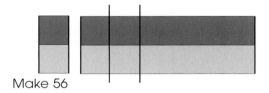

Make 56

3 Place a 2"-wide unit with a blue square at top, right sides together, on a 2"-wide unit with a green square at top. Sew the units together, as shown. Press. Repeat to make a total of 28 four-patch squares.

Make 28

Sashing

Cutting

Light Print Fabric:
Cut 4—2" strips for sashing

Medium Green Print Fabric:
Cut 4—2" strips for sashing

1 Sew a light print fabric strip to a medium green print fabric strip to make one strip set. Repeat to make a total of four strip sets.

Make 4

2 Cut each strip set into 6-1/2"-wide units for a total of 20 sashing units.

Make 20

3 With right sides together and the light print fabric toward the block, sew a sashing unit to the left and right sides of two Cornerstone blocks.

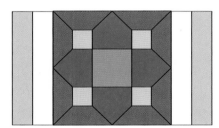

Make 2

4 With right sides together and the medium green print fabric toward the block, sew a sashing unit to the left and right sides of the remaining Cornerstone block. This is the center block.

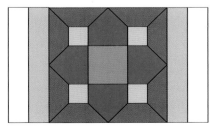

Make 1

5 Making sure the medium green print squares are opposite the medium green print sashing units, sew a four-patch square to each end of the remaining sashing units.

6 Sew a sashing/four-patch square unit to the top and bottom edges of the Cornerstone blocks, making sure the colors match. Sew a second sashing/four-patch square unit to the top and bottom edges of each block.

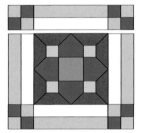 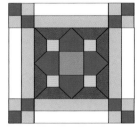

Make 2   Make 1

7 Sew the three blocks together.

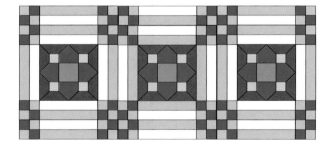

8 Center and sew the remaining sashing/four-patch square unit to the left and right side edges of the outer blocks.

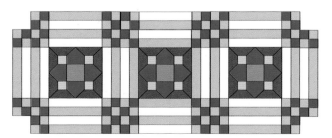

8 To angle the corners of the runner, cut the corner four-patch squares at 45-degree angles, leaving 1/4" seam allowances.

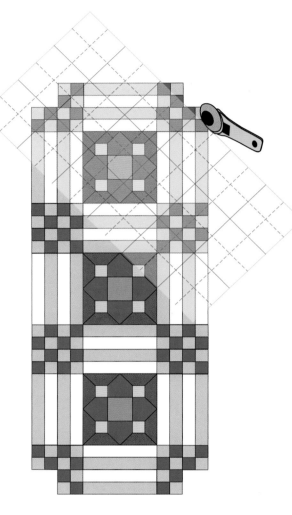

Backing & Binding

Cutting

Medium Floral Print Fabric:
Cut 1 strip 3" wider than the runner top for backing

Dark Blue Print Fabric:
Cut 4—2-1/4" strips for binding

1 Layer the runner top, batting, and backing. Quilt and bind the table runner as desired.

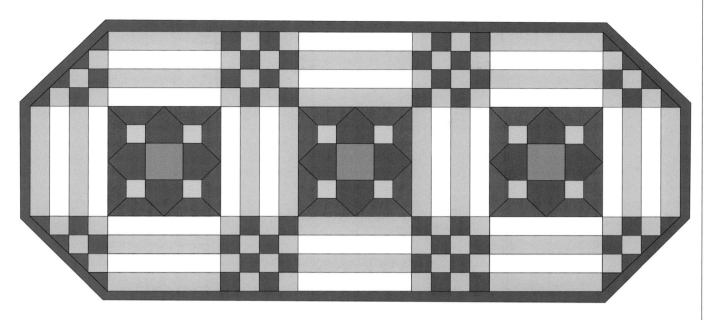

Cornerstone
table runner

table runner block and color option

*Substitute your favorite Pieced Appliqué™ block in the Cornerstone Table Runner.
We used the St. Gregory's Cross block on page 54.*

Pieced by Jeri Simon; machine quilted by Lynn Witzenburg.

Cornerstone
place mats

12" x 18"

Note: *All yardage requirements are based on
44"-wide fabric, NOT pre-washed.
Measurements include 1/4" seam allowance.*

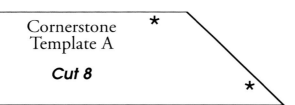

Cornerstone
Template A

Cut 8

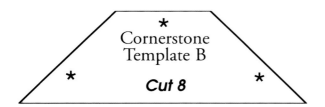

Cornerstone
Template B

Cut 8

Cornerstone
Pieced Appliqué™ Blocks

Follow the directions on pages 45-46 to make
two Cornerstone Pieced Appliqué™ blocks.

Paper Templates:
Cut 8 of Template A and
8 of Template B

Four-Patch Squares

Cutting

Medium Green Print Fabric:
Cut 4—2" strips

Dark Blue Print Fabric:
Cut 2—2" strips
Sub-cut each strip in half

Make 16 Four-Patch Squares

The Cornerstone block is framed with four sashing strips and a four-patch square in each corner. The framed block unit makes up the center of the place mat. Instructions are for two place mats.

1 Sew a 2"-wide dark blue print strip to a 2"-wide medium green print strip to make one strip set. Repeat to make a total of four strip sets.

Make 4

2 Cut each strip set into 2"-wide units for a total of 32 units.

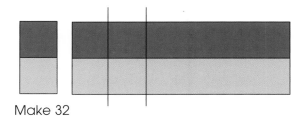

Make 32

3 Place a 2"-wide unit with a blue square at top, right sides together, on a 2"-wide unit with a green square at top. Sew the units together, as shown. Press. Repeat to make a total of 16 four-patch squares.

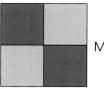

Make 16

Sashing

Cutting

Light Print Fabric:
Cut 4—2" strips for sashing

Medium Green Print Fabric:
Cut 4—2" strips for sashing

1 Sew a light print fabric strip to a medium green print fabric strip to make one strip set. Repeat to make a total of three strip sets.

Make 3

2 Cut each strip set into 6-1/2"-wide units for a total of 12 sashing units.
With right sides together and the light print fabric toward the block, sew a sashing unit to the left and right sides of one Cornerstone block.

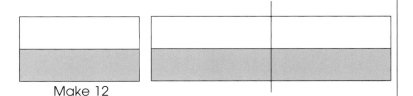

Make 12

3 With right sides together and the light print fabric toward the block, sew a sashing unit to the left and right sides of the second Cornerstone block.

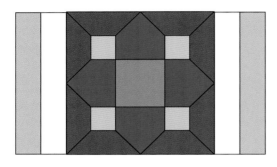

4 Making sure the medium green print squares are opposite the medium green print sashing units, sew a four-patch square to each end of the remaining sashing units.

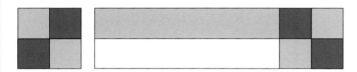

5 Sew a sashing/four-patch square unit to the top and bottom edges of the two Cornerstone blocks, making sure the colors match.

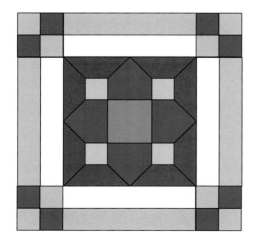

6 Center and sew the remaining sashing/four-patch square units to the side edges of each block.

7 To angle the corners of the place mats cut the corner four-patch squares at 45-degree angles, leaving 1/4" seam allowances.

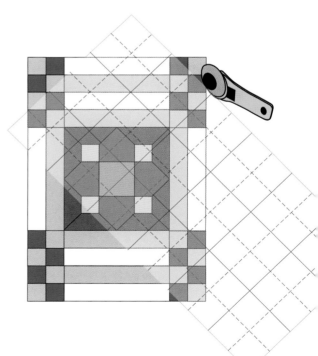

Backing & Binding

Cutting

Medium Floral Print Fabric:
Cut 2—18" x 24" rectangles
for backing

Dark Blue Print Fabric:
Cut 4—2-1/4" strips for binding

Note: *I gave my machine quilter 1/2 yard of backing fabric. She pinned and quilted both place mats to this piece. Ask your machine quilter how she would like these pieces prepared.*

1 Layer the place mat top, batting, and backing. Quilt and bind the place mats as desired.

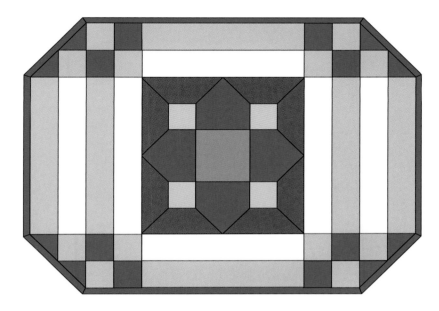

Cornerstone
place mat

St. Gregory's Cross
throw
62-1/2" x 62-1/2"

Two simple templates and the Pieced Appliqué™ technique combine to make a beautiful throw featuring the St. Gregory's Cross block.

Designed by Penny Haren; pieced by Barb Campolo. Machine quilted by Cheryl Lorence.

Fabrics

Floral Print Fabric:
1 yard for Pieced Appliqué™ blocks and outer border

Medium Blue Print Fabric:
1-5/8 yards for Pieced Appliqué™ blocks, four-patch squares, sashing strips, border squares, inner border, and binding

Dark Green Print Fabric:
2/3 yard for Pieced Appliqué™ blocks, four-patch squares, sashing strips, and corner squares

White Print Fabric:
1-1/3 yards for sashing strips

Light Floral Print Fabric #1:
4 yards for Pieced Appliqué™ blocks and backing

Light Floral Print Fabric #2:
Fat quarter for Pieced Appliqué™ blocks

Light Blue Print Fabric:
Fat quarter for Pieced Appliqué™ blocks

Medium Green Print Fabric:
Fat quarter for Pieced Appliqué™ blocks

Refer to General Instructions on pages 8-19 before beginning this project.

Note: *All yardage requirements are based on 44"-wide fabric, NOT pre-washed. Measurements include 1/4" seam allowance.*

St. Gregory's Cross Pieced Appliqué™ Blocks

Cutting

Floral Print Fabric:
#1—Cut 9—2-1/2" Squares

Medium Blue Print Fabric:
#2—Cut 36—2-1/2" Squares

Dark Green Print Fabric:
#3—Cut 36—2-1/2" Squares

Light Floral Print Fabric #1:
Scraps to cut 20 of Appliqué A for Block 1

Light Floral Print Fabric #2:
Scraps to cut 16 of Appliqué A for Block 2

Light Blue Print Fabric:
Scraps to cut 20 of Appliqué B for Block 1

Medium Green Print Fabric:
Scraps to cut 16 of Appliqué B for Block 2

Paper Templates:
Cut 36 of Template A and 36 of Template B

Make 9—St. Gregory's Cross Pieced Appliqué™ Blocks
(5 Medium Blue/Dark Green and 4 Dark Green/Medium Blue)

St. Gregory's Cross
Template A

Cut 36

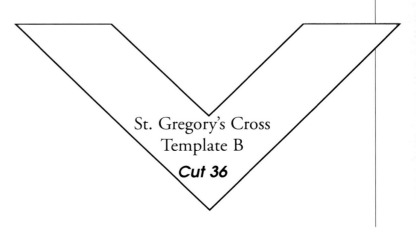

St. Gregory's Cross
Template B

Cut 36

Piecing

This block consists of 17 pieces.

> **Note:** *Try fussy cutting the center light print 2-1/2" square and the A appliqués.*

1 Following the nine-patch foundation block directions on page 38, make a nine-patch with the #1 floral print square (center); the #2 medium blue print squares (corners); and the #3 dark green print squares. Press the seams open. This will be the foundation for Block 1.

Block 1 foundation

2 Make a nine-patch with the #1 floral print square (center); the #3 dark green print squares (corners); and the #2 medium blue print squares. Press the seams open. This will be the foundation for Block 2.

Block 2 foundation

3 Glue 20 A paper templates to the wrong side of a scrap of light foral print fabric #1. Trim the fabric EXACTLY 1/4" away from all sides of the templates. Turn two opposite sides of each appliqué. Do not turn the other two sides.

Template A (Block 1)

> **Note:** ⋆ *on paper templates indicates sides of fabric to be turned.*

4 Glue 16 A paper templates to the wrong side of a scrap of light foral print fabric #2. Trim the fabric EXACTLY 1/4" away from all sides of the templates. Turn two opposite sides of each appliqué. Do not turn the other two sides.

Template A (Block 2)

5 Glue the wrong side of the appliqués in place on the pieced nine-patch block. The raw edges of the appliqués will be covered by the B appliqués.

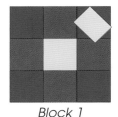

Block 1   *Block 2*

6 Glue 20 B paper templates to the wrong side of a scrap of light blue print fabric. Trim the fabric EXACTLY 1/4" away from all sides of the templates. Turn the two sides that form right triangles. Do not turn the two short, straight sides.

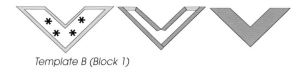

Template B (Block 1)

7 Glue 16 B paper templates to the wrong side of a scrap of medium green print fabric. Trim the fabric EXACTLY 1/4" away from all sides of the templates. Turn the two sides that form right triangles. Do not turn the two short, straight sides.

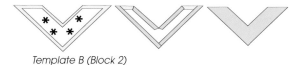

Template B (Block 2)

8 Glue the wrong side of the appliqués in place on the pieced block. Place the raw edges of the appliqués even with the raw edges of the pieced block.

Block 1

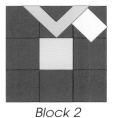

Block 2

9 Appliqué in place, leaving raw edges open. Follow directions on pages 16-17 to remove paper templates and glue. Press.

10 Repeat steps 1-9 to make a total of five Block 1 and four Block 2.

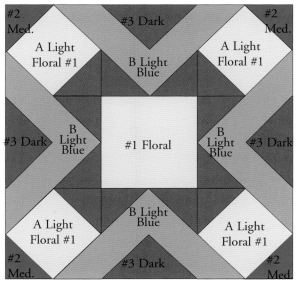

#2 Med.   #3 Dark   #2 Med.
A Light Floral #1   B Light Blue   A Light Floral #1
#3 Dark   B Light Blue   #1 Floral   B Light Blue   #3 Dark
A Light Floral #1   B Light Blue   A Light Floral #1
#2 Med.   #3 Dark   #2 Med.

Block 1

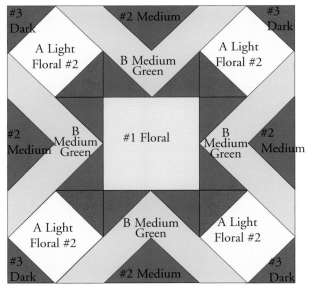

#3 Dark   #2 Medium   #3 Dark
A Light Floral #2   B Medium Green   A Light Floral #2
#2 Medium   B Medium Green   #1 Floral   B Medium Green   #2 Medium
A Light Floral #2   B Medium Green   A Light Floral #2
#3 Dark   #2 Medium   #3 Dark

Block 2

Four-Patch Squares

Cutting

Medium Blue Print Fabric:
Cut 2—2" strips

Dark Green Print Fabric:
Cut 2—2" strips

Make 40 Four-Patch Squares

1 Sew a 2" medium blue print fabric strip to a 2" dark green print fabric strip to make one strip set. Repeat to make a second strip set.

Make 2

2 Cut each strip set into 2"-wide units for a total of 80 units.

Make 80

3 Place a 2"-wide unit with a medium blue square at top, right sides together, on a 2"-wide unit with a dark green square at top. Sew the units together, as shown. Press. Repeat to make a total of 40 four-patch squares.

Make 40

Block Sashing

Cutting

White Print Fabric:
Cut 7—2" strips

Medium Blue Print Fabric:
Cut 4—2" strips

Dark Green Print Fabric:
Cut 3—2" strips

1 Sew a white print fabric strip to a medium blue print fabric strip to make one strip set. Repeat to make a total of four white/medium blue strip sets.

Make 4

2 Sew a white print fabric strip to a dark green print fabric strip to make one strip set. Repeat to make a total of three white/dark green strip sets.

Make 3

3 Cut each strip set into 6-1/2"-wide units for a total of 20 white/medium blue print sashing units and 16 white/dark green print sashing units.

4 With right sides together and the white print fabric toward the blocks, sew a white/medium blue print sashing unit to the top and bottom edge of each Block 1.

5 With right sides together and the white print fabric toward the blocks, sew a white/dark green print sashing unit to the top and bottom edge of each Block 2.

6 Making sure the medium blue print squares are opposite the medium blue print sashing units, sew a four-patch square to each end of 10 white/medium blue print sashing units.

Make 10

7 Making sure the dark green print squares are opposite the dark green print sashing units, sew a four-patch square to each end of eight white/dark green print sashing units.

Make 8

8 Sew a white/medium blue print sashing/four-patch square unit to the side edges of each Block 1, making sure the colors match.

Make 5 Block 1

9 Sew a white/dark green print sashing/four-patch square unit to the side edges of each Block 2, making sure the colors match.

Make 4 Block 2

Throw Center Sashing

Cutting

White Print Fabric:
Cut 9—3-1/2" strips
Sub-cut **4 strips** into 12—12-1/2" strips

Dark Green Print Fabric:
Cut 4—3-1/2" corner squares

1 Lay out two Block 1, one Block 2, and two 12-1/2" sashing strips, as shown. Sew the row together. Repeat to make a total of two rows.

Make 2 rows

2 Lay out two Block 2, one Block 1, and two 12-1/2" sashing strips, as shown. Sew the row together.

Make 1 row

3 Sew together the remaining 12-1/2" white print sashing strips and the four-patch squares, as shown.

4 Lay out the block rows and sashing strips, as shown, below. Sew together.

5 Measure each side of the throw center. Trim the four 3-1/2" white print strips to the same length as the center's sides.

6 Sew a strip to the side edges of the throw center.

7 Sew a 3-1/2" dark green print corner square to each end of the remaining white print strips.

8 Sew the white print/dark green sashing strips to the top and bottom edges of the throw center.

Borders

Cutting

Medium Blue Print Fabric:
Cut 5—2" strips for inner border
Sub-cut **1 strip** into 4—10" strips
Cut 4—6" border squares

Floral Print Fabric:
Cut 6—6" strips for outer border
Sub-cut **2 strips** into 2—20" strips

Note: *In our throw, the border print is directional. Therefore, we bought 1-1/2 yards and cut 2—6" strips the LENGTH of the piece. We then cut 4—6" strips the width of the remaining fabric, which measured approximately 28". These pieced segments were used for the top and bottom borders. The following instructions were written for a non-directional print.*

1 Sew a 10" strip to the four remaining medium blue print strips.

2 Measure the side edges of the throw center. Cut two medium blue print strips to those measurements. Sew the strips to the throw's side edges.

3 Measure the top and bottom edges of the throw center, including the the side inner border strips. Cut two medium blue print strips to those measurements. Sew the strips to the top and bottom edges of the throw center.

4 Sew a 20" strip to the four remaining floral print strips.

5 Measure the edges of the throw center. Trim four floral print strips to those measurements.

6 Sew a strip to the side edges of the throw center.

7 Sew a 6" medium blue border square the remaining floral print strips.

8 Sew the strips to the top and bottom edges of the throw center.

Backing & Binding

Cutting

Medium Blue Print Fabric:
Cut 7—2-1/4" strips for binding

1 Layer the backing fabric, batting, and throw top. Quilt and bind as desired.

St. Gregory's Cross
throw

Half-Square Triangles Foundation Block

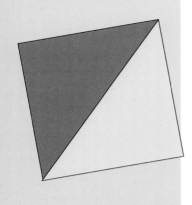

A half-square triangle is a square that consists of two ninety-degree triangles pieced on the longest side.

Note: *Generally, when making half-square triangles, the squares should be cut 7/8" larger than the finished block. Since you are sewing bias seams, the sewing and pressing tend to distort the shape of your finished square. Therefore, I add 2" so that I can square them up to the correct size after stitching and pressing.*

Make a sample block to learn the technique before cutting the fabric for your project.

FABRICS

2—4" Squares of Light Fabric

2—4" Squares of Dark Fabric

PIECING

1 Place a light fabric square, right sides together, on top of a dark fabric square. Draw a line across the diagonal. Be sure to use a pencil or a marking tool that is water soluble. Ink may bleed onto your quilt when you wash it. Repeat with the other set of squares.

Note: *It is easier to draw the line from the center out in both directions so you don't wrinkle the corners.*

2 Stitch a seam 1/4" on each side of the drawn line. Cut on the drawn line. Repeat with the other set of squares.

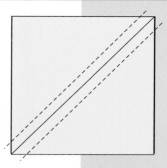

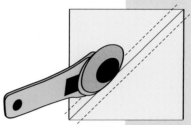

3 Open the half-square triangles and press the seams open. Each set of squares will make two half-square triangle units. These blocks will be slightly larger than 3-1/2".

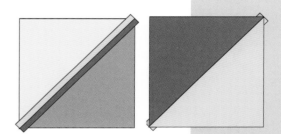

4 Place the 6" Miniature Ruler on the upper left corner of the right side of the square. The diagonal line marking on the ruler should be placed on the seam line. Trim the top and left side.

5 Turn the block so the uncut edges are on the top and left side. Place the 6" Miniature Ruler so the diagonal line is placed on the seam line and the 2-7/8" markings are even with the square on the right and bottom sides. Trim the top and left side. The finished square now measures to 2-7/8".

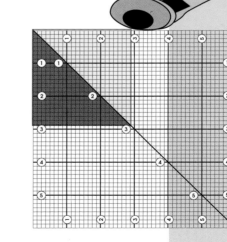

Grandmother's Choice
table topper
29-3/4" x 51"

With the half-square triangles foundation block and the Pieced Appliqué™ setting triangles you can make a stunning table topper or mantle cover.

Designed by Penny Haren; pieced by Barb Campolo. Machine quilted by Cheryl Lorence.

Fabrics

Light Blue Print Fabric:
Scrap or Fat Quarter for
Pieced Appliqué™ blocks

Light Gold Print Fabric:
1/2 yard for Pieced Appliqué™
blocks and setting triangles

Medium Blue Print Fabric:
1/2 yard for setting blocks

Medium Brown Print Fabric:
1-5/8 yards for backing

Dark Blue Print Fabric:
2/3 yard for Pieced Appliqué™
blocks, setting blocks,
and setting triangles

Dark Brown Print Fabric:
1-1/8 yards for Pieced Appliqué™
blocks, setting triangles,
and prairie points

Muslin or Extra Fabric:
2 yards for lining

*Refer to General Instructions on pages 8-19
before beginning this project.*

Note: All yardage requirements
are based on 44"-wide fabric,
NOT pre-washed. Measurements include
1/4" seam allowance.

---

*
Grandmother's
Choice
Template A *
Cut 20

Grandmother's Choice Pieced Appliqué™ Blocks

Cutting

Light Gold Print Fabric:
#1—Cut 10—4" Squares

Light Blue Print Fabric:
#2—Cut 20—1-3/4" x 2-7/8" Rectangles

Dark Blue Print Fabric:
#3—Cut 5—1-3/4" Square

Dark Brown Print Fabric:
#4—Cut 10—4" Squares
Scraps to Cut 20 of Appliqué A

Paper Templates:
Cut 20 of Template A

**Make 5—Grandmother's Choice
Pieced Appliqué™ Blocks**

Piecing

This block consists of 17 pieces.

1 Following the half-square triangles
foundation block instructions on page 62
make four half-square triangles
with the #1 light gold print fabric
and the #4 dark brown print fabric.
Press the seams open. Trim these half-
square triangles to 2-7/8" squares.

2 Following the nine-
patch foundation
block directions on
page 38 make a
nine-patch with the
#3 dark blue print
square (center); the
trimmed half-square
triangles (corners); and the #2 light blue
print rectangles. Press the seams open.

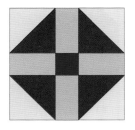

3 Glue the C paper templates to the wrong side of the dark blue print fabric. Trim the fabric EXACTLY 1/4" away from all sides of the templates. Turn the two short sides of each appliqué.

Template C

4 Glue the wrong side of the appliqués in place on the triangle so the turned point of appliqué C touches the turned point of appliqué B. The raw edge of appliqué C should be even with the raw edge of the triangle.

5 Appliqué in place. Follow directions on pages 16-17 to remove paper templates and glue. Press.

6 Repeat Steps 1 - 6 to make 12 border triangles.

Prairie Points and Table Topper Top

Cutting

Dark Brown Print Fabric:
Cut 5—9" squares for prairie points
Cut 2—9" strips

Note: *You may adjust the width of these strips to custom fit the topper to your needs. Don't forget to add 1/2" to this width to allow for the seam allowances. I made mine to fit my mantel which is 8-1/2" wide. You may cut these strips the width of a buffet or the top of an upright piano. Be creative.*

1 To assemble the center of the table topper, lay out the 5 Grandmother's Choice blocks, 12 quarter-square triangle setting blocks, 12 side setting triangles, and the corner setting triangles together in diagonal rows, as shown. The setting triangles are over-sized.

2 Sew the rows together. Trim the side setting triangles 1/4" away from the points of the quarter-square triangle setting blocks on all sides.

3 To make prairie points fold each 9" dark brown print square in half diagonally. Fold in half again to form a triangle.

4 With raw edges aligned, sew the dark brown print triangles to the quarter-square triangle setting blocks at the bottom of the table topper.

5 Join the two 9" dark brown print strips together along the 9" edges. You need a 9" x 51-1/2" strip.

6 Sew the strip to the top edge of the table topper.

Lining

Cutting

Muslin or Extra Fabric:
Cut (or piece together)
1—32" x 57" rectangle

1 Layer the table topper, a thin batting, and the pieced rectangle. Quilt as desired, making sure to quilt only up to the outer seam allowances of the top, side, and bottom edges, omitting the dark brown print prairie points. To avoid bulk, trim away excess batting and lining fabric.

Backing

Cutting

Medium Brown Print Fabric:
Cut (or piece together)
1—26" x 53" rectangle

1 With right sides together and the back of the table topper facing you, center and sew the table topper to the medium brown print rectangle, sewing first the top edge and then the side edges. Do not sew the bottom edge. Trim the top and side seam allowances even. Turn the table topper right side out. Turn under the bottom edge of the lining and hand sew in place.

Grandmother's Choice

table topper

Pinwheel Foundation Block

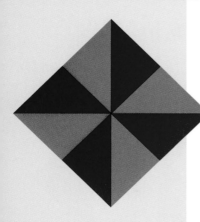

A pinwheel is made from four half-square triangles.

Make a sample block to learn the technique before cutting the fabric for your quilt.

PIECING

1 Following the half-square triangle directions on page 62, make four half-square triangles.

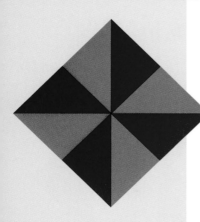

FABRICS

4—4" Squares of Light Fabric

4—4" Squares of Dark Fabric

2 Lay out the four half-square triangles to form a pinwheel. It is possible to sew a mirror image of this block and have the blades of your pinwheel "blowing" in the other direction. Be careful.

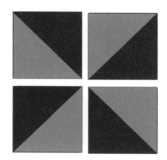

3 Place the half-square triangles in the second column, right sides together, over the first column, matching the seams. Place a dab of glue on the seam so it doesn't shift while sewing.

4 Sew these seams, one after the other, by chain-piecing them on the sewing machine.

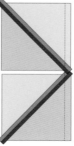

5 Press the seams open. Check and make sure that the points of the triangles match 1/4" in from the outer edge. If they do not match now, the center of the pinwheel will not match after the final seam is sewn.

6 Place the right column over the left column, right sides together, matching the center seam. Use a dab of glue to make sure that nothing shifts when stitching. Sew this final seam. Press the seam open.

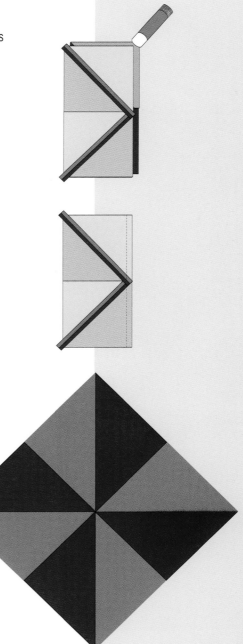

Shaded Trail
table runner
13" x 47-1/2"

Have fun substituting other blocks and seasonal colors in this simple table runner and place mat setting.

Designed and pieced by Penny Haren. Machine quilted by Cheryl Lorence.

Fabrics

Light Cream Print Fabric:
1/3 yard for Pieced Appliqué™ blocks and Flying Geese

Medium Rust Print Fabric:
Fat quarter or 1/4 yard for Pieced Appliqué™ blocks and Flying Geese

Medium Gold Print Fabric:
Fat quarter or 1/4 yard for Pieced Appliqué™ blocks and Flying Geese

Dark Green Print Fabric:
1/2 yard for Flying Geese and border

Dark Rust Print Fabric:
1-1/2 yards for backing and binding

Refer to General Instructions on pages 8-19 before beginning this project.

Note: *All yardage requirements are based on 44"-wide fabric, NOT pre-washed. Measurements include 1/4" seam allowance.*

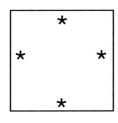

Shaded Trail
Template A

Cut 4

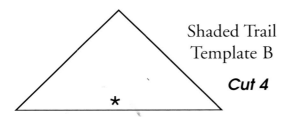

Shaded Trail
Template B

Cut 4

Shaded Trail
Pieced Appliqué™ Blocks

Cutting

Light Cream Print Fabric:
Scraps to Cut 4 of Appliqué A
& 4 of Appliqué B

Medium Rust Print Fabric:
#1—Cut 2—3-1/2" Squares
#2—Cut 2—1-1/2" x 2-3/4" Rectangles
#3—Cut 2—1-1/2" x 3-3/4" Rectangles

Medium Gold Print Fabric:
#4—Cut 2—3-1/2" Squares

#5—Cut 2—1-1/2" x 2-3/4" Rectangles
#6—Cut 2—1-1/2" x 3-3/4" Rectangles

Paper Templates:
Cut 4 of Template A & 4 of Template B

**Make 1—Shaded Trail
Pieced Appliqué™ Block**

Piecing
This block consists of 24 pieces.

1 Following the half-square triangles foundation block instructions on page 62, make four half-square triangles from the #1 medium rust print fabric squares and #4 medium gold print fabric squares. Press the seams open.

2 Trim the finished half-square triangles to 2-3/4".

3 Follow the pinwheel foundation block directions on page 70 to make a pinwheel from the four half-square triangles. Press all seams open. The pinwheel should measure 5".

4 Sew a #2 medium rust print fabric rectangle to a #5 medium gold print fabric rectangle along the 1-1/2" side. Press the seam open. Make a total of two units.

5 Sew these units to opposite sides of the pinwheel, matching the seams. Press the seams open.

6 Sew a #3 medium rust print fabric rectangle to a #6 medium gold print fabric rectangle along the 1-1/2" side. Press the seam open. Make a total of two units.

7 Sew these units to the other two sides of the pinwheel, matching the seams. Press the seams open. Trim this pieced block to 6-1/2".

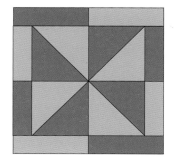

8 Glue the A paper templates to the wrong side of a scrap of light print fabric. Trim the fabric 1/4" away from the templates on all sides. Turn all four sides of the A appliqués.

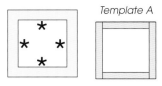

Template A

Note: ✱ *on paper templates indicates sides of fabric to be turned.*

9 Place the A appliqués on the pieced block, matching the points of the square to the seam lines.

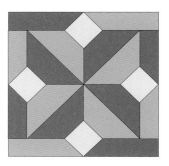

10 Glue the B paper templates to the wrong side of a scrap of light print fabric. Trim the fabric 1/4" away from the templates on all sides. Turn the long side of the B appliqués.

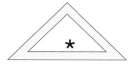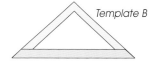

Template B

11 Place the B appliqués on the pieced block. The raw edges of the appliqués should be placed even with the raw edges of the corner of the pieced block.

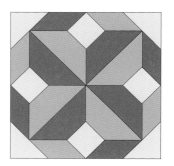

12 Appliqué in place, leaving the raw edges of the B appliqué open. Follow the directions on pages 16-17 to remove paper templates and glue. Press.

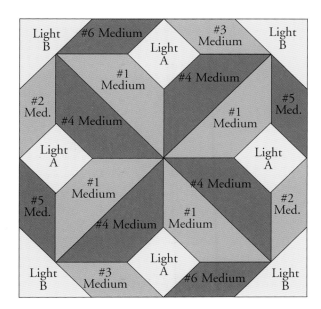

Flying Geese Variation

Cutting

Medium Rust Print Fabric:
Cut 4—2-1/2" x 7-1/2" rectangles
Cut 4—2-1/2" x 9-1/2" rectangles

Medium Gold Print Fabric:
Cut 4—2-1/2" x 7-1/2" rectangles
Cut 4—2-1/2" x 9-1/2" rectangles

Dark Green Print Fabric:
Cut 2—2-1/2" x 6-1/2" rectangles
Cut 4—2-1/2" x 7-1/2" rectangles
Cut 6—2-1/2" x 9-1/2" rectangles

Light Cream Print Fabric:
Cut 12—4-3/8" squares

Piecing

1 Sew a 6-1/2" dark green print rectangle to opposite sides of the Shaded Trail block. Press the seams away from the Shaded Trail block.

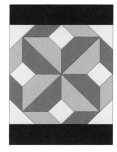

2 Sew a 9-1/2" dark green print rectangle to the other two sides - starting at opposite corners. These pieces are shorter than the length of the side. Press the seams away from the Shaded Trail block. When the strips are added, the outside edge will be jagged. It will be trimmed 1/4" away from the points of the Shaded Trail block when the entire table runner is pieced.

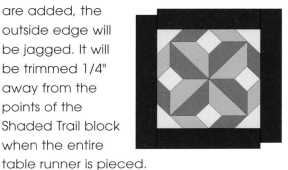

3 With wrong sides together, fold the light cream print squares in half on the diagonal.

4 Place the raw edges of these triangles even with the right angle of the pieced center. The fold should be placed on the point of the Shaded Trail block. The raw edges of these folded units will be inserted in the seams when each set of rectangles is added.

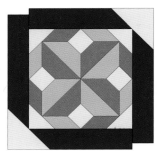

Note: By inserting the folded triangles instead of piecing them, they can be placed perfectly and no bias edges are involved. These light triangles are a perfect setting for a beautiful embroidery design. By folding the fabric, there is a stable foundation for the embroidery and the double layer of fabric guarantees that the darker fabrics will not

shadow through. You may choose to appliqué these folds or just catch the edges when machine quilting the finished project.

5 Sew a 7-1/2" medium gold print rectangle to opposite sides of the Shaded Trail block. Press the seams away from the Shaded Trail block.

6 Sew a 9-1/2" medium gold print rectangle to the other two sides – starting at the right angle. These pieces are shorter than the length of the side. Press the seams away from the Shaded Trail block.

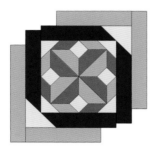

7 Continue adding triangles and strips until the entire table runner is pieced. Ending with a set of dark green print rectangles.

8 With a water soluble marker, draw a line 1/4" away from the point of the Shaded Trail block. The 4-1/2" line on the ruler should extend through the center of the Shaded Trail block and the points of the light fabric triangles. Make any adjustments necessary so the same line on the ruler is placed through these points. Draw a line the entire length of the piece and repeat for the other side.

9 Measure the distance between these two lines at several different points along the length of the pieced table runner. They should be the same width - approximately 9". Stay stitch right inside this drawn line.

Note: *Stay stitching is sewing a straight line right inside the drawn line. The threads in th_ stitched line do not stretch and will stop the bias edge from stretching when the jagged edge is trimmed.*

10 Trim on the drawn line.

Border

Cutting
Dark Green Print Fabric:
Cut 2—2-1/2" strips
for top and bottom borders

1 Remove the selvages from the strips. Center and sew a strip to the top and bottom of the pieced table runner.

2 Trim the end of these border strips even with the angled ends of the table runner.

Backing & Binding

Cutting

Dark Rust Print Fabric:
Cut 1—18-1/2" x 54" strip the length of the fabric for the backing

Note: *I left a 1-1/2 yard backing piece intact and gave it to my machine quilter along with the place mats. She quilted them both to this piece of backing. If you are not going to make both projects, you can cut the bias binding out of the other half.*

Cut 1—27" square; sub-cut into 2-1/2" bias strips for binding

Note: *I used a plaid for the binding and cut it on the bias so it would appear "on point" and add interest to the completed project. I also cut this binding to 2-1/2" instead of 2-1/4" because I wanted more of it to show. Therefore, I sewed the binding to the back of the piece and hand stitched it to the front of the table runner.*

1 Layer the runner top, batting, and runner backing together. Quilt and bind as desired.

Shaded Trail
place mats

13" x 20"

Designed and pieced by Penny Haren. Machine quilted by Cheryl Lorence.

Note: All yardage requirements are based on 44"-wide fabric, NOT pre-washed. Measurements include 1/4" seam allowance.

Fabrics

Fabrics and instructions will make two place mats.

Light Cream Print Fabric:
Fat quarter or 1/4 yard for Pieced Appliqué™ blocks and Flying Geese

Medium Rust Print Fabric:
Fat quarter or 1/4 yard for Pieced Appliqué™ blocks and Flying Geese

Medium Gold Print Fabric:
Fat quarter or 1/4 yard for Flying Geese

Dark Green Print Fabric:
1/3 yard for Pieced Appliqué™ blocks, Flying Geese and border

Dark Rust Print Fabric:
1-1/3 yards for backing and binding

Refer to General Instructions on pages 8-19 before beginning this project.

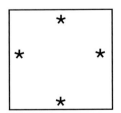

Shaded Trail
Template A

Cut 8

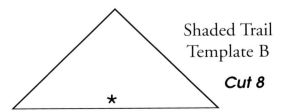

Shaded Trail
Template B

Cut 8

Shaded Trail
Pieced Appliqué™ Blocks

Cutting

Light Cream Print Fabric:
Scraps to Cut 8 of Appliqué A
& 8 of Appliqué B

Medium Rust Print Fabric:
#1—Cut 4—3-1/2" Squares
#2—Cut 4—1-1/2" x 2-3/4" Rectangles
#3—Cut 4—1-1/2" x 3-3/4" Rectangles

Dark Green Print Fabric:
#4—Cut 4—3-1/2" Squares
#5—Cut 4—1-1/2" x 2-3/4" Rectangles
#6—Cut 4—1-1/2" x 3-3/4" Rectangles

Paper Templates:
Cut 8 of Template A &
8 of Template B

**Make 2—Shaded Trail
Pieced Appliqué™ Blocks**

Piecing

This block consists of 24 pieces.

1 Following the half-square triangles foundation block instructions on page 62, make four half-square triangles from the #1 medium rust print fabric squares and #4 dark green print fabric squares. Press the seams open.

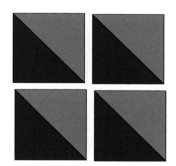

2 Trim the finished half-square triangles to 2-3/4".

3 Follow the pinwheel foundation block directions on page 70 to make a pinwheel from the four half-square triangles. Press all seams open. The pinwheel should measure 5".

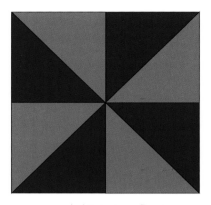

4 Sew a #2 medium rust print fabric rectangle to a #5 dark green print fabric rectangle along the 1-1/2" side. Press the seam open. Make a total of two units.

5 Sew these units to opposite sides of the pinwheel, matching the seams. Press the seams open.

6 Sew a #3 medium rust print fabric rectangle to a #6 dark green print fabric rectangle along the 1-1/2" side. Press the seam open. Make a total of two units.

7 Sew these units to the other two sides of the pinwheel, matching the seams. Press the seams open. Trim this pieced block to 6-1/2".

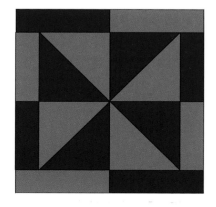

8 Glue the A paper templates to the wrong side of a scrap of light cream print fabric. Trim the fabric 1/4" away from the templates on all sides. Turn all four sides of the A appliqués.

Template A

Note: ★ *on paper templates indicates sides of fabric to be turned.*

9 Place the A appliqués on the pieced block, matching the points of the square to the seam lines.

10 Glue the B paper templates to the wrong side of a scrap of light print fabric. Trim the fabric 1/4" away from the templates on all sides. Turn the long side of the B appliqués.

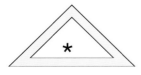 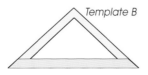

Template B

11 Place the B appliqués on the pieced block. The raw edges of the appliqués should be placed even with the raw edges of the corner of the pieced block.

12 Appliqué in place, leaving the raw edges of the B appliqué open. Follow the directions on pages 16-17 to remove paper templates and glue. Press.

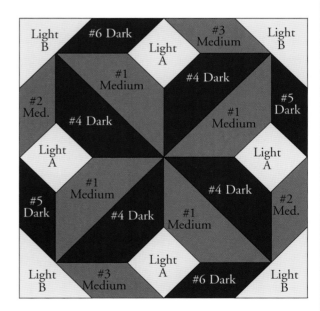

Flying Geese Variation

Cutting

Medium Rust Print Fabric:
Cut 4—2-1/2" x 7-1/2" rectangles
Cut 4—2-1/2" x 9-1/2" rectangles

Medium Gold Print Fabric:
Cut 4—2-1/2" x 6-1/2" rectangles
Cut 4—2-1/2" x 9-1/2" rectangles

Dark Green Print Fabric:
Cut 4—2-1/2" x 7-1/2" rectangles
Cut 4—2-1/2" x 9-1/2" rectangles

Light Cream Print Fabric:
Cut 8—4-3/8" squares

Piecing

1 Sew a 6-1/2" medium gold
print rectangle to opposite
sides of the Shaded Trail
block Press the seams
away from the Shaded
Trail block.

2 Sew a 9-1/2" medium gold print rectangle
to the other two sides - starting at opposite
corners. These pieces are shorter than the
length of the side. Press the seams away
from the Shaded Trail block. When the strips
are added, the outside
edge will be jagged. It
will be trimmed 1/4"
away from the points of
the Shaded Trail block
when the entire place
mat is pieced.

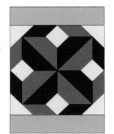

3 With wrong sides together, fold the light
cream print squares in half on the diagonal.

4 Place the raw edges
of the triangles even
with the right angle of
the pieced center. The
fold should be placed
on the point of the
Shaded Trail block. The

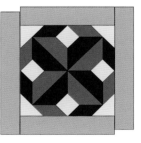

raw edges of these folded units will be
inserted in the seams when each set of
rectangles is added.

Note: *By inserting these folded triangles
instead of piecing them, they can be
placed perfectly and no bias edges are
involved. These light triangles are a perfect
setting for a beautiful embroidery design. By
folding the fabric, there is a stable foundation for the embroidery and the double
layer of fabric guarantees that the darker
fabrics will not shadow through. You may
choose to appliqué these folds or just
catch the edges when machine quilting
the finished project.*

5 Sew a 7-1/2" medium rust print rectangle
to opposite sides of the Shaded Trail block.
Press the seams away from the Shaded
Trail block.

6 Sew a 9-1/2" medium rust print rectangle to
the other two sides – starting at the right
angle. These pieces are shorter than the
length of the side. Press the seams away
from the Shaded Trail block.

7 Add a set of dark green rectangles in the
same manner.

8 With a water soluble marker, draw a line
1/4" away from the point of the Shaded Trail
block. The 4-1/2" line on the ruler should
extend through the center of the Shaded
Trail block and the points of the light fabric
triangles. Make any adjustments necessary
so the same line on the ruler is placed
through these points. Draw a line the entire
length of the piece and repeat for the
other side.

9 Measure the distance between these two lines at several different points along the length of the pieced place mat. They should be the same width - approximately 9". With a water soluble marker, draw a line 1/4" away from the point of the light cream print on each end. Stay stitch right inside these drawn lines. Trim on the drawn line.

Note: Stay stitching is sewing a straight line right inside the drawn line. The threads in this stitched line do not stretch and will stop the bias edge from stretching when the jagged edge is trimmed.

Border

Cutting

Dark Green Print Fabric:
Cut 2—2-1/2" strips for top and bottom borders; sub-cut these strips in half

1 Remove the selvages from the strips. Center and sew a strip to the top and bottom of the pieced place mat.

2 Trim the end of these border strips even with the angled ends of the place mat.

Backing & Binding

Cutting

Dark Rust Print Fabric:
Cut 1—19" strip the width of the fabric for backing

Note: This is enough for both place mats.

1—27" square; sub-cut into 2-1/2" bias strips for binding

Note: I used a plaid for the binding and cut it on the bias so it would appear "on point" and add interest to the completed project. I also cut this binding to 2-1/2" instead of 2-1/4" because I wanted more of it to show. Therefore, I sewed the binding to the back of the piece and hand stitched it to the front of the place mat.

1 Layer the place mat top, batting, and backing together. Quilt and bind as desired.

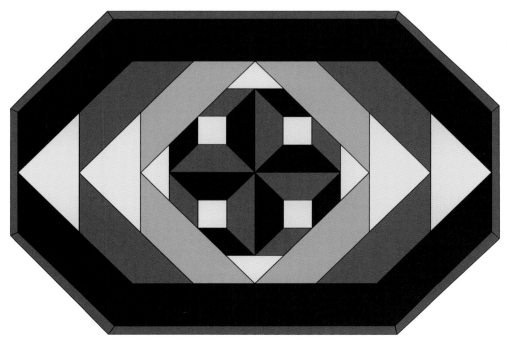

Shaded Trail
place mats

Kaleidoscope Foundation Block

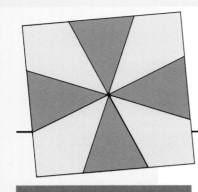

A Kaleidoscope Block is cut from a pinwheel block.

Make a sample block to learn the technique before cutting the fabric for your quilt.

FABRICS

Cut 2—6" Squares from Light Fabric

Cut 2—6" Squares from Dark Fabric

PIECING

1 Following the directions on page 62, make four half-square triangles from the 6" squares of light and dark fabrics. Trim these finished half-square triangles to 5".

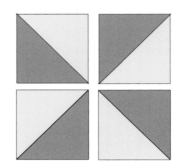

2 Sew four half-square triangles together to form a pinwheel. Press the seams open.

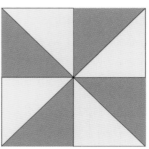

CUTTING THE KALEIDOSCOPE:

3 Glue the kaleidoscope template to the wrong side of the pinwheel block, matching the lines on the template to the seam lines of the pinwheel. The kaleidoscope block instructions state which fabric should be on the corners. Place the template accordingly.

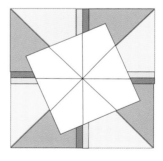

4 Place the 6-1/2" Creative Grids™ *Square It Up & Fussy Cut* ruler on top of the template so that the 1/4" seam extends beyond the template on all sides.

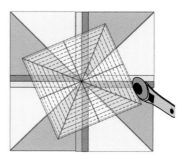

Borders & Binding

Cutting

Dark Paisley Print Fabric:
Cut 2—3" strips for borders
Cut 3—2-1/4" strips for binding

1 Measure the two long sides of the table runner center. Add 1" to the measurement. Cut the two 3" strips to the measurement calculated.

2 Sew one of the strips to each long side of the table runner. Press.

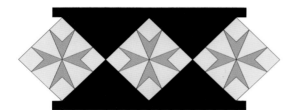

3 Sew the remaining 3" strips to each end of the table runner. Trim away excess fabric.

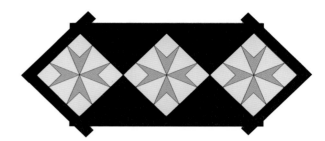

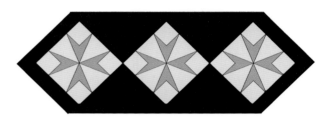

4 Layer table runner top, batting, and backing together. Quilt and bind as desired.

table runner block and color option

Substitute your favorite Pieced Appliqué™ block in the Star of the East Table Runner. We used the Advanced Liberty Star block on page 32.

Pieced by Sue Voegtlin; machine quilted by Lynn Witzenburg.

Bright Hopes Foundation Block

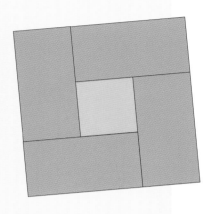

A Bright Hopes block consists of a center square surrounded by four rectangles of equal size. This method eliminates the need to sew an inset point.

Make a sample block to learn the technique before cutting the fabric for your quilt.

PIECING

1 Lay the center square on one of the rectangles, right sides together. Sew a partial seam approximately 1- 3/4" long. Press the seam open.

2 Place the seamed edge on a 2-1/2" x 4-1/2" rectangle of fabric, right sides together. Sew along the 4-1/2" length. Press the seam open.

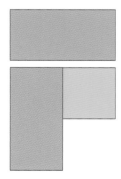

3 Place the seamed edge on a 2-1/2" x 4-1/2" rectangle of fabric, right sides together. Sew along the 4-1/2" length. Press the seam open.

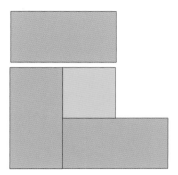

4 Place the seamed edge on a 2-1/2" x 4-1/2" rectangle of fabric, right sides together. Sew along the 4-1/2" length. Press the seam open.

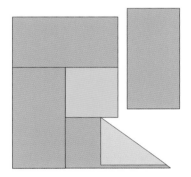

5 Finish sewing the partial seam to connect the first 2-1/2" x 4-1/2" rectangle. Press the seam open.

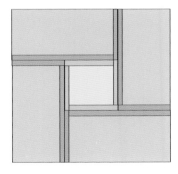 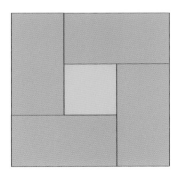

Whirligigs
bulletin board
22" x 30"

You'll have a fun bulletin board with the Pieced Appliqué™ Whirligigs block, but just as easily, you can adjust this pattern to become a table topper or table runner. Use your favorite Pieced Appliqué™ blocks and play.

Designed by Penny Haren; pieced by Barb Campolo. Machine quilted by Cheryl Lorence.

Fabrics

Light Print Fabric:
Fat quarter for Pieced Appliqué™ blocks and button covers

Dark Print Fabric:
3/4 yard for Pieced Appliqué™ blocks and border

Medium Print Fabric:
Scraps for Pieced Appliqué™ blocks

White Print Fabric:
2/3 yard for setting blocks

Muslin or Extra Fabric:
1 yard for backing

Muslin or Extra Fabric:
1 yard to cover back of bulletin board (optional)

OTHER MATERIALS
Two packages of
black medium rick rack
12—3/4" diameter buttons
22" x 30" piece of
1/2" thick foam insulation
Large T pins
Two picture hangers
Refer to General Instructions on pages 8-19 before beginning this project.

Note: *All yardage requirements are based on 44"-wide fabric, NOT pre-washed. Measurements include 1/4" seam allowance.*

Whirligigs
Pieced Appliqué™ Blocks

Cutting

Light Print Fabric:
Cut 24 of Appliqué A

Medium Print Fabric:
#1—Cut 6—3-1/2" Square

Dark Print Fabric:
#2—Cut 24—2" x 5" Rectangles

Paper Templates:
Cut 24 of Template A

Make 6—Whirligigs Pieced Appliqué™ Blocks

Piecing

This block consists of 9 pieces.

1. Following the Bright Hopes foundation block directions on page 88, piece a Bright Hopes block from the #1 medium print square and the #2 dark print rectangles. Press the seams toward the dark print rectangles.

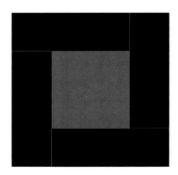

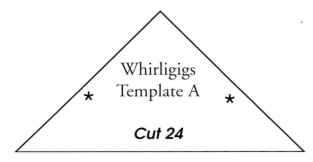

Whirligigs
Template A

Cut 24

2 Glue the A paper templates to the wrong side of a scrap of the light print fabric. Trim the fabric 1/4" away from the templates on all sides. Turn the two short sides of each appliqué.

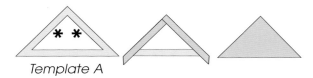

Template A

Note: * on paper templates indicates sides of fabric to be turned.

3 Glue the wrong side of the A appliqués in place on the pieced Bright Hopes block. The raw edge of the appliqués should be placed even with the raw edges of the Bright Hopes block.

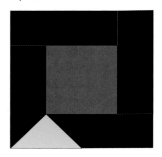

4 Appliqué in place, leaving raw edges open. Follow directions on pages 16-17 to remove paper templates and glue. Press.

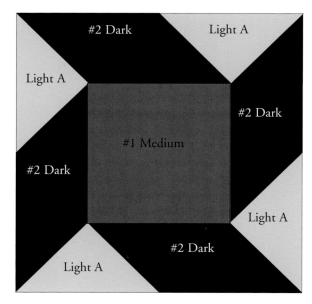

5 Repeat Steps 1-4 to make a total of 6 Whirligigs blocks.

Setting Blocks, Side Setting Triangles, and Corner Setting Triangles

Cutting

Note: *The triangles will be over-sized.*

White Print Fabric:
Cut 2—11" squares; sub-cut both ways on the diagonal for side setting triangles
Cut 2—7" squares; sub-cut once on the diagonal for corner setting triangles
Cut 2—6-1/2" squares for setting squares

Black Rick Rack:
Cut 4—6-1/2" pieces for setting blocks
Cut 16—4" pieces for side setting corners and triangles

Make 2 Setting Blocks, 6 Side Setting Triangles, and 4 Corner Triangles

Piecing

1 Using two pieces of black rick rack form a "t" in the center of a white print square. Tack the rick rack in place in the center of the square and pin at the outer edges. Repeat to make a total of two setting blocks.

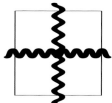

Make 2

2 Place two pieces of rick rack 3-1/4" down from the short side of each side setting triangle. Pin in place. Do not tack the loose ends in place. They will be tacked down after the side setting triangles are trimmed.

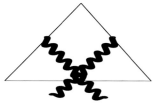

Make 6

3 Fold the long edge of the corner setting triangle in half and place the rick rack on this fold. Pin in place on the longest side of the triangle. Do not tack the loose ends in place. They will be tacked down after the corner setting triangles are trimmed.

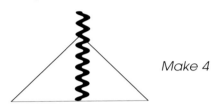

Make 4

4 To assemble the center of the bulletin board, lay out the 6 Whirligigs blocks, the 6 side setting triangles, and the 4 corner triangles together in diagonal rows, as shown.

5 Sew the rows together to complete the center of the bulletin board – butting seams.

6 Trim the corner and side setting triangles 1/4" away from the points of the Whirligigs blocks. Tack the rick rack in place along the outside edge of the pieced center.

Border

Cutting

Dark Print Fabric:
Cut 2—4-1/2" x 17-1/2" strips
Cut 2—4-1/2" x 34" strips

1 Sew the 4-1/2" x 17-1/2" strips to the side edges of the bulletin board center. Press.

2 Sew the 4-1/2" x 34" strips to the top and bottom edges of the bulletin board center. Press.

3 Quilt the bulletin board cover as desired. Edge-stitch around the entire cover. There is no need for binding.

4 Cut 1-1/2" circles of the medium print fabric. Run a gathering stitch around the outside edge of the circle. Place a button in the center of this fabric circle and pull the thread to gather the fabric around it. Tack in place. Sew a covered button to each rick rack intersection on the setting blocks.

Note: I used a double strand of Pearl Cotton and tied a knot that showed on the top. Simply go through the fabric and then through the holes that are in the buttons.

5 Using T pins, stretch the bulletin board cover on the foam insulation board, first pinning the center of each border to the 1/2" edge of the board and working out to the corners. Turn the board to the wrong side and, if desired, stretch and pin a piece of fabric or muslin to the back. Pull the borders over the board's edges, pinning them in place as you go. Remove the edge pins. Tack the picture hangers to the back of the board.

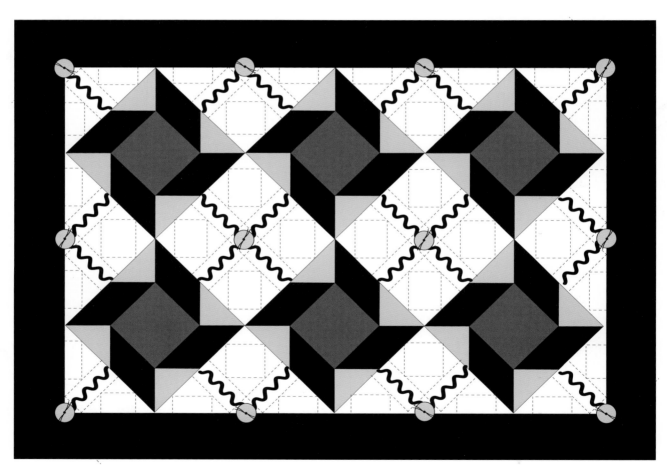

Whirligigs
bulletin board

Penny Haren's
Pieced Appliqué™

Introducing Innovative Techniques for
Creating Perfect Blocks for Successful

Lover's Knot

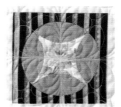

Kitty's World

Hummingbird

Bow Tie

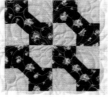

King David's Crown

1941 Nine-Patch

Attic Windows

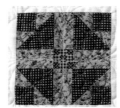

Grandmother's Choice

Old Windmills

United No Longer

Eight-Pointed Star

Missouri Daisy

Star of the East

Joseph's Coat

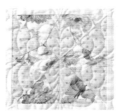

Mill and Stars

The Arrow Star

Jeri's Star

St. Gregory's Cross

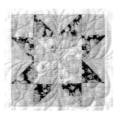

Sarah's Choice

Debby's
Nine-Patch Art

Boston
Uncommon

Sue's Hot
Cross Buns

Keri's Star

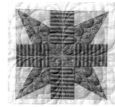

Whirligigs

Windblown Square

Penny Haren's
Pieced Appliqué™
More Blocks & Projects

Liberty Star

Homemaker

Cross Roads

True Lover's Knot

Kansas Dug-Out

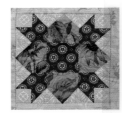
Weathervane

Cornerstone

Farmer's Daughter

Laurel's Wreath

Clay's Choice

Shaded Trail

LeMoyne Star

Lone Star

E-Z Quilt

Purple Cross

Spider Web

Jewel Star

Spools

Baton Rouge

Saw Tooth

Rosemary's Star

Rose Trellis

Jed's Star

Rae's Star